g

GEOMETRY

Math Preparation Guide

This comprehensive guide illustrates every geometric
principle, formula, and problem type tested on the GMAT.
Understand and master the intricacies of shapes, planes,
lines, angles, and objects.

Geometry GMAT Preparation Guide

10-digit International Standard Book Number: 0-9748069-4-3
13-digit International Standard Book Number: 978-0-9748069-4-5

Note: *GMAT, Graduate Management Admission Test, Graduate Management Admission Council,* and *GMAC* are all registered trademarks of the Graduate Management Admission Council which neither sponsors nor is affiliated in any way with this product.

7 GUIDE INSTRUCTIONAL SERIES

Math GMAT Preparation Guides

Number Properties (ISBN: 0-9748069-0-0)

FDP's: Fractions, Decimals, & Percents (ISBN: 0-9748069-1-9)

Equations, Inequalities, & VIC's (ISBN: 0-9748069-3-5)

Word Translations (ISBN: 0-9748069-2-7)

Geometry(ISBN: 0-9748069-4-3)

Verbal GMAT Preparation Guides

Critical Reasoning & Reading Comprehension (ISBN: 0-9748069-6-X)

Sentence Correction (ISBN: 0-9748069-5-1)

HOW OUR GMAT PREP BOOKS ARE DIFFERENT

One of our core beliefs at Manhattan GMAT is that a curriculum should be more than just a guidebook of tricks and tips. Scoring well on the GMAT requires a curriculum that builds true content knowledge and understanding. Skim through this guide and this is what you will see:

You will *not* find page after page of guessing techniques.

Instead, you will find a highly organized and structured guide that actually teaches you the content you need to know to do well on the GMAT.

You *will* find many more pages-per-topic than in all-in-one tomes.

Each chapter covers one specific topic area in-depth, explaining key concepts, detailing in-depth strategies, and building specific skills through Manhattan GMAT's *In-Action* problem sets (with comprehensive explanations). Why are there 7 guides? Each of the 7 books (5 Math, 2 Verbal) covers a major content area in extensive depth, allowing you to delve deep into each topic. In addition, you may purchase only those guides that pertain to your weaknesses.

This guide is challenging - it asks you to do more, not less.

It starts with the fundamental skills, but does not end there; it also includes the *most advanced content* that many other prep books ignore. As the average GMAT score required to gain admission to top business schools continues to rise, this guide, together with the simulated online practice exams and bonus question bank included with your purchase, provides test-takers with the depth and volume of advanced material essential for succeeding on the GMAT's computer adaptive format.

This guide is ambitious - developing mastery is its goal.

Developed by Manhattan GMAT's staff of REAL teachers (all of whom have 99th percentile official GMAT scores), our ambitious curriculum seeks to provide test-takers of all levels with an in-depth and carefully tailored approach that enables our students to achieve mastery. If you are looking to learn more than just the "process of elimination" and if you want to develop skills, strategies, and a confident approach to any problem that you may see on the GMAT, then our sophisticated preparation guides are the tools to get you there.

HOW TO ACCESS YOUR ONLINE RESOURCES

Please read this entire page of information, all the way down to the bottom of the page! This page describes WHAT online resources are included with the purchase of this book and HOW to access these resources.

[**If you are a registered Manhattan GMAT student** and have received this book as part of your course materials, you have AUTOMATIC access to ALL of our online resources. This includes all simulated practice exams, question banks, and online updates to this book. To access these resources, follow the instructions in the Welcome Guide provided to you at the start of your program. Do NOT follow the instructions below.]

If you have purchased this book, your purchase includes 1 YEAR OF ONLINE ACCESS to the following:

> **3 Simulated Online Practice Exams**
>
> **Bonus Online Question Bank for GEOMETRY**
>
> **Online Updates to the Content in this Book**

The 3 full-length practice exams included with the purchase of this book are delivered online using Manhattan GMAT's proprietary online test engine. All questions included in the exams are unique questions written by Manhattan GMAT's expert instructors, all of whom have scored in the 99th percentile on the Official GMAT. The exams are non-adaptive and include questions of varying difficulty levels. At the end of each exam you will receive a score, an analysis of your results, and the opportunity to review detailed explanations for each question. You may choose to take the exams timed or untimed.

The Bonus Online Question Bank for Geometry consists of 25 extra practice questions (with detailed explanations) that test the variety of Geometry concepts and skills covered in this book. These questions provide you with extra practice *beyond* the problem sets contained in this book. You may use our online timer to practice your pacing by setting time limits for each question in the bank.

The content contained in this book is updated periodically to ensure that it reflects the GMAT's most current trends. All updated information, including any known errors or changes to this book, is posted online. You will be able to view all updates to this book upon registering for your online access.

<u>**Important Note:**</u> The 3 online exams included with the purchase of this book are the SAME exams that you receive upon purchasing ANY book in Manhattan GMAT's 7 Book Preparation Series. (See the bottom front cover of this book for a list of all 7 titles.) On the other hand, the Bonus Online Question Bank for GEOMETRY is a unique resource that you receive ONLY with the purchase of this specific title.

To access the online resources listed above, you will need this book in front of you and you will need to register your information online. This book includes access to the above resources for ONE PERSON ONLY.

To register and start using your online resources, please go online to the following URL:

http://www.manhattangmat.com/access.cfm   (Double check that you have typed this in accurately!)

Your 1 year of online access begins on the day that you register at the above URL.

TABLE OF CONTENTS

g

g

Chapter 1
of
GEOMETRY

POLYGONS

In This Chapter . . .

POLYGONS

A polygon is defined as a closed shape formed by line segments. The polygons tested on the GMAT include:

Three-sided shapes: Triangles.
Four-sided shapes: Quadrilaterals.
Other polygons with *n* sides (where *n* is five or more).

This section will focus on polygons of four or more sides. In particular, the GMAT emphasizes quadrilaterals—or four-sided polygons—including trapezoids, parallelograms, and special parallelograms, such as rhombuses, rectangles, and squares.

Polygons are two-dimensional shapes; they lie in a plane. The GMAT tests your ability to work with different measurements associated with polygons. The measurements you must be adept with are: (1) interior angles, (2) perimeter, and (3) area.

The GMAT also tests your knowledge of three-dimensional shapes formed from polygons, particularly rectangular solids and cubes. The measurements you must be adept with are (1) surface area and (2) volume.

> A polygon is a closed shape formed by line segments.

Quadrilaterals: An Overview

The most common non-triangle polygon tested on the GMAT is the quadrilateral (any four-sided polygon). Almost all GMAT polygon problems involve the special types of quadrilaterals shown below.

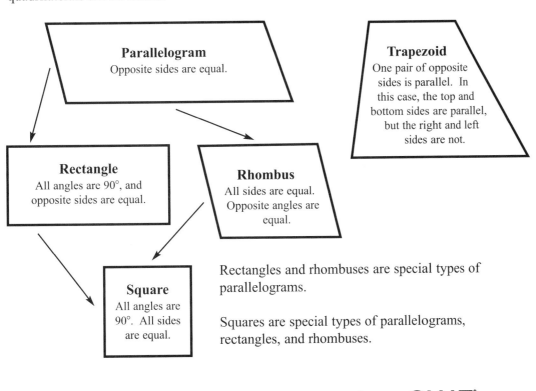

Parallelogram
Opposite sides are equal.

Trapezoid
One pair of opposite sides is parallel. In this case, the top and bottom sides are parallel, but the right and left sides are not.

Rectangle
All angles are 90°, and opposite sides are equal.

Rhombus
All sides are equal. Opposite angles are equal.

Square
All angles are 90°. All sides are equal.

Rectangles and rhombuses are special types of parallelograms.

Squares are special types of parallelograms, rectangles, and rhombuses.

Polygons and Interior Angles

The sum of the interior angles of a given polygon is dependent on the number of sides that the polygon has. The following chart displays the relationship between the type of polygon and the sum of its interior angles:

Notice that the sum of the interior angles of a polygon follows a regular pattern that is dependent on *n*, the number of sides of the polygon. Specifically, the sum of the angles of a polygon is always 2 less than *n* (the number of sides) times 180°.

Polygon	# of sides	Sum of Interior Angles
Triangle	3	180°
Quadrilateral	4	360°
Pentagon	5	540°
Hexagon	6	720°

This can be expressed with the following formula:

$$(n - 2)180 = \text{Sum of Interior Angles of a Polygon}$$

As this is a four-sided polygon, the sum of its interior angles is $(4 - 2)180 = 2(180) = 360°$. Alternately, note that a quadrilateral can be cut into two triangles; thus, the sum of the angles $= 2(180) = 360°$.

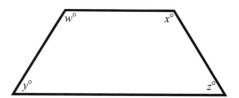

As this is a six-sided polygon, the sum of its interior angles is $(6 - 2)180 = 4(180) = 720°$. Alternately, note that a hexagon can be cut into four triangles; thus, the sum of the angles $= 4(180) = 720°$.

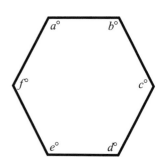

*Manhattan*GMAT*Prep
the new standard

Polygons and Perimeter

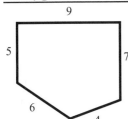

The perimeter refers to the distance around a polygon, or the sum of the lengths of all the sides. The amount of fencing needed to surround a yard would be equivalent to the perimeter of that yard (the sum of all the sides).

The perimeter of the pentagon to the left is:
9 + 7 + 4 + 6 + 5 = **31**.

Polygons and Area

The area refers to the space inside a polygon. Area is delineated in square units, such as cm^2 (square centimeters) or m^2 (square meters) or ft^2 (square feet). The amount of space that a garden occupies is the area of that garden.

On the GMAT, there are two polygon area formulas you MUST know:

1) Area of a TRIANGLE: $\dfrac{\textbf{Base} \times \textbf{Height}}{\textbf{2}}$

The base refers to the bottom side of the triangle. The height refers to a line that is perpendicular (at a 90° angle) to the base.

You must memorize the formulas for the area of a triangle and for the area of the quadrilaterals shown in this section.

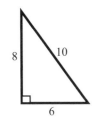

In this triangle, the base is 6 and the height (perpendicular to the base) is 8. The area = (6 × 8) ÷ 2 = 48 ÷ 2 = 24.

$$\frac{6 \cdot 8}{2} = \frac{48}{2} = 24$$

In this triangle, the base is 12, but the height is not shown. Neither of the other two sides of the triangle is perpendicular to the base. In order to find the area of this triangle, we would first need to determine the height, which is represented by the dotted line.

$a^2 + b^2 = c^2 \qquad 12^2 + b^2 = 100$
$144 + b^2 = 100$
$b^2 = 244$
$b = \sqrt{244}$

2) Area of a RECTANGLE: **Length × Width**

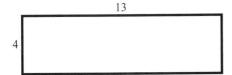

The length of this rectangle is 13, and the width is 4. Therefore, the area = 13 × 4 = 52.

The GMAT will occasionally ask you to find the area of a polygon more complex than a simple triangle or rectangle. The following formulas can be used to find the areas of other types of quadrilaterals:

3) Area of a TRAPEZOID = $\dfrac{(\text{Base}_1 + \text{Base}_2) \times \text{Height}}{2}$

Note that the height refers to the line perpendicular to the two bases. In the trapezoid to the right, base$_1$ = 18, base$_2$ = 6, and the height = 8. The area = $8 \times (18 + 6) \div 2 = 96$. Another way to think about this is to take the *average* of the two bases and multiply it by the height.

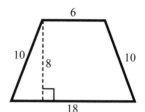

> Notice that most of these formulas involve finding a base and a line perpendicular to that base (a height).

4) Area of any PARALLELOGRAM = **Base × Height**

Note that the height refers to the line perpendicular to the base. In the parallelogram to the right, the base = 5 and the height = 8. The area is $5 \times 8 = 40$.

5) Area of a RHOMBUS = $\dfrac{\text{Diagonal}_1 \times \text{Diagonal}_2}{2}$

Note that the diagonals of a rhombus are perpendicular. The area of this rhombus is $\dfrac{6 \times 8}{2} = \dfrac{48}{2} = 24$.

Although these formulas are very useful to memorize for the GMAT, you may notice that all of the above shapes can actually be cut up into some combination of rectangles and right triangles. Therefore, if you forget the area formula for a particular shape, simply cut the shape into rectangles and right triangles, and find the areas of these individual pieces. For example:

*Manhattan*GMAT*Prep
the new standard

3 Dimensions: Surface Area

The GMAT tests two particular three-dimensional shapes formed from polygons: the rectangular solid and the cube. Note that a cube is just a special type of rectangular solid.

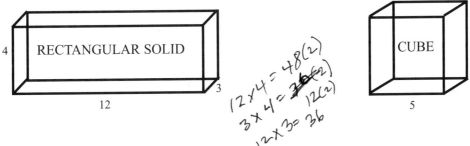

The surface area of a three-dimensional shape is the amount of space on the surface of that particular object. For example, the amount of paint that it would take to fully cover a rectangular box could be determined by finding the surface area of that box. As with simple area, surface area is delineated using square units such as inches^2 (square inches) or ft^2 (square feet).

> **Surface Area = the SUM of the areas of ALL the faces**

Both a rectangular solid and a cube have **six faces**.

To determine the surface area of a rectangular solid, you must find the area of each face. Notice, however, that in a rectangular solid, the front and back faces have the same area, the top and bottom faces have the same area, and the two side faces have the same area. In the solid above, the area of the front face is equal to $12 \times 4 = 48$. Thus, the back face also has an area of 48. The area of the bottom face is equal to $12 \times 3 = 36$. Thus, the top face also has an area of 36. Finally, each side face has an area of $3 \times 4 = 12$. Therefore, the surface area, or the sum of the areas of all six faces $= 48(2) + 36(2) + 12(2) = 192$.

To determine the surface area of a cube, you only need the length of one side. We can see from the cube above that a cube is made of six square surfaces. First, find the area of one face: $5 \times 5 = 25$. Then, multiply by six to account for all the faces: $6 \times 25 = 150$.

You don't need to memorize a formula for surface area. Simply find the sum of all the faces.

3 Dimensions: Volume

The volume of a three-dimensional shape is the amount of "stuff" it can hold. For example, the amount of liquid that a rectangular milk carton holds can be determined by finding the volume of the carton. Volume is delineated using cubic units such as inches^3 (cubic inches) or ft^3 (cubic feet).

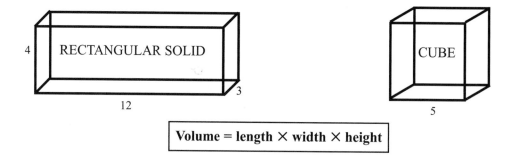

4 | RECTANGULAR SOLID | | CUBE

12 | 3 | 5

Volume = length × width × height

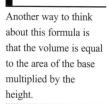

By looking at the rectangular solid above, we can see that the length is 12, the width is 3, and the height is 4. Therefore, the volume is $12 \times 3 \times 4 = 144$.

In a cube, all three of the dimensions—length, width, and height—are identical. Therefore, knowing the measurement of just one side of the cube is sufficient for finding the volume. In the cube above, the volume is $5 \times 5 \times 5 = 125$.

 Beware of the GMAT volume trick:

> **How many books, each with a volume of 100 in^3, can be packed into a crate with a volume of 5,000 in^3?**

It is tempting to answer: 50 books (since $50 \times 100 = 5,000$). However, this is incorrect, because we don't know the exact dimensions of each book! One book might be $5 \times 5 \times 4$, while another book might be $20 \times 5 \times 1$. Even though both have a volume of 100 in^3, they have different rectangular shapes. Without knowing the exact shapes of all the books, there is no way to tell if they would all fit into the crate. Remember, when fitting 3-dimensional objects into other 3-dimensional objects, knowing the respective volumes is not enough; we must know the specific dimensions (length, width, and height) of each object to determine if it can fit.

Sidebar: Another way to think about this formula is that the volume is equal to the area of the base multiplied by the height.

Problem Set (Note: Figures are not drawn to scale.)

1. Frank the Fencemaker needs to fence in a rectangular yard. He fences in the entire yard, except for one 40-foot side of the yard. The yard has an area of 280 square feet. How many feet of fence does Frank use?

2. A pentagon has three sides with length x, and two sides with the length $3x$. If x is $\frac{2}{3}$ of an inch, what is the perimeter of the pentagon?

3. ABCD is a quadrilateral, with AB parallel to CD (see figure). E is a point between C and D such that AE represents the height of ABCD, and E is the midpoint of CD. If AB is 4 inches long, AE is 5 inches long, and the area of triangle AED is 12.5 square inches, what is the area of ABCD?

    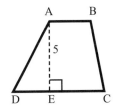

4. A rectangular tank needs to be coated with insulation. The tank has dimensions of 4 feet, 5 feet, and 2.5 feet. Each square foot of insulation costs $20. How much will it cost to cover the tank with insulation?

5. Triangle ABC (see figure) has a base of $2y$, a height of y, and an area of 49. What is y?

    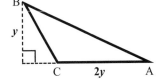

6. 40 percent of Andrea's living room floor is covered by a Mexican carpet that is 4 feet by 9 feet. What is the area of her living room floor?

7. If the perimeter of a rectangular flower bed is 30 feet, and its area is 44 square feet, what is the length of each of its shorter sides?

8. There is a rectangular parking lot with a length of $2x$ and a width of x. What is the ratio of the perimeter of the parking lot to the area of the parking lot, in terms of x?

9. A rectangular solid has a square base, with each side of the base measuring 4 meters. If the volume of the solid is 112 cubic meters, what is the surface area of the solid?

10. ABCD is a parallelogram (see figure). The ratio of DE to EC is 1:3. AE has a length of 3. If quadrilateral ABCE has an area of 21, what is the area of ABCD?

    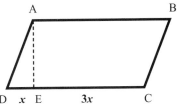

11. A swimming pool has a length of 30 meters, a width of 10 meters, and an average depth of 2 meters. If a hose can fill the pool at a rate of .5 cubic meters per minute, how many hours will it take the hose to fill the pool?

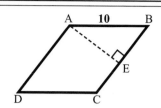

12.   ABCD is a rhombus (see figure). ABE is a right triangle.
       AB is 10 meters. CE and EB are in the ratio of 2 to 3.
       What is the area of trapezoid AECD?

13.   A Rubix cube has an edge of 5 inches. What is the
       ratio of the cube's surface area to its volume?

14.   If the length of an edge of Cube A is one third the length of an edge of Cube B, what is
       the ratio of the volume of Cube A to Cube B?

15.   ABCD is a square picture frame (see figure). EFGH is a
       square inscribed within ABCD as a space for a picture. The
       area of EFGH (for the picture) is equal to the area of the
       picture frame (the area of ABCD minus the area of EFGH).
       If AB = 6, what is the length of EF?

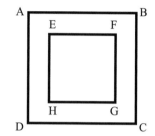

1. **54 feet:** We know that one side of the yard is 40 feet long; let's call this the length. We also know that the area of the yard is 280 square feet. In order to determine the perimeter, we must know the width of the yard.

$$A = l \times w$$
$$280 = 40w$$
$$w = 280 \div 40 = 7 \text{ feet}$$

Frank fences in the two 7-foot sides and one of the 40-foot sides. $40 + 2(7) = 54$.

2. **6 inches:** The perimeter of a pentagon is the sum of its five sides: $x + x + x + 3x + 3x = 9x$. If x is 2/3 of an inch, the perimeter is $9(2/3)$, or 6 inches.

3. **35 in²:** If E is the midpoint of C, then CE = DE = x. We can determine the length of x by using what we know about the area of triangle AED.

$$A = \frac{b \times h}{2} \qquad 12.5 = \frac{5x}{2}$$

$$25 = 5x$$
$$x = 5$$

Therefore, the length of CD is $2x$, or 10.

To find the area of the trapezoid, use the formula: $A = \dfrac{b_1 + b_2}{2} \times h$

$$= \frac{4 + 10}{2} \times 5$$

$$= 35 \text{ in}^2$$

4. **$1,700:** To find the surface area of a rectangular solid, sum the individual areas of all six faces:

Top and Bottom:	5×4	$= 20$	$\rightarrow$ 2×20	$= 40$
Side 1:	5×2.5	$= 12.5$	$\rightarrow$ 2×12.5	$= 25$
Side 2:	4×2.5	$= 10$	$\rightarrow$ 2×10	$= 20$

$$40 + 25 + 20 = 85 \text{ ft}^2$$

To cover the entire tank, it will cost $85 \times \$20 = \$1,700$.

5. **7:** The area of a triangle is equal to half the base times the height. Therefore,

$$\frac{2y(y)}{2} = 49$$

$$y^2 = 49$$
$$y = 7$$

6. **90 ft²:** The area of the Mexican carpet is equal to $l \times w$, or 36 ft². Set up a percent table or a proportion to find the area of the whole living room floor:

$$\frac{40}{100} = \frac{36}{x} \qquad \text{Cross-multiply to solve.}$$

$$40x = 3600$$
$$x = 90 \text{ ft}^2$$

7. **4:** Set up equations to represent the area and perimeter of the flower bed:

$$A = l \times w \qquad\qquad P = 2(l + w)$$

Then, substitute the known values for the variables A and P:

$$44 = l \times w \qquad\qquad 30 = 2(l + w)$$

Solve the two equations with the substitution method:

$$l = \frac{44}{w}$$

$$30 = 2(\frac{44}{w} + w)$$

Multiply the entire equation by $\frac{w}{2}$.

$$15w = 44 + w^2$$
$$w^2 - 15w + 44 = 0$$
$$(w - 11)(w - 4) = 0$$
$$w = \{4, 11\}$$

Solving the quadratic equation yields two solutions: 4 and 11. Since we are looking only for the length of the shorter side, the answer is 4.

8. $\frac{3}{x}$: If the length of the parking lot is $2x$ and the width is x, we can set up a fraction to represent the ratio of perimeter to area as follows:

$$\frac{\text{perimeter}}{\text{area}} = \frac{2(2x + x)}{(2x)(x)} = \frac{6x}{2x^2} = \frac{3}{x}$$

9. **144 m²:** The volume of a rectangular solid equals (length) × (width) × (height). If we know that the length and width are both 4 meters long, we can substitute values into the formulas as shown:

$$112 = 4 \times 4 \times h$$
$$h = 7$$

To find the surface area of a rectangular solid, sum the individual areas of all six faces:

| Top and Bottom: | $4 \times 4 = 16$ | → | $2 \times 16 = 32$ |
| Sides: | $4 \times 7 = 28$ | → | $4 \times 28 = 112$ |

$$32 + 112 = 144 \text{ m}^2$$

10. **24:** First, break quadrilateral ABCE into 2 pieces: a 3 by $3x$ rectangle, and a right triangle with a base of x and a height of 3. The area of quadrilateral ABCE, therefore, is:

$$(3 \times 3x) + \frac{3 \times x}{2} = 9x + 1.5x = 10.5x$$

If ABCE has an area of 21, then $21 = 10.5x$, and $x = 2$. Quadrilateral ABCD is a parallelogram; its area is equal to (base) × (height), or $4x \times 3$. Substitute the known value of 2 for x and simplify:

$$A = 4(2) \times 3 = 24$$

11. **20 hours:** The volume of the pool is (length) × (width) × (height), or $30 \times 10 \times 2 = 600$ cubic meters. Use a standard work equation, $RT = D$, where D represents the total work of 600 m³.

$$.5t = 600$$
$$t = 1200 \text{ minutes}$$

Convert this to hours by dividing by 60: $1200 \div 60 = 20$ hours.

12. **56 m²:** To find the area of a trapezoid, we need the lengths of both parallel bases and the height. If ABCD is a rhombus, then AD = AB = 10. This gives us the length of the first base, AD. We also know that CB = 10 and $\dfrac{CE}{EB} = \dfrac{2}{3}$. Use the unknown multiplier concept to find the length of the

second base, CE:
$$2x + 3x = 10$$
$$5x = 10$$
$$x = 2$$

Thus, CE = 2x = 2(2) = 4.

Now all that remains is the height of the trapezoid, AE. If you recognize that AE forms the long leg of a right triangle (ABE), you can use the Pythagorean Theorem to find the length of AE:
$$6^2 + b^2 = 10^2$$
$$b = 8$$

The area of the trapezoid is: $\dfrac{b_1 + b_2}{2} \times h = \dfrac{10 + 4}{2} \times 8 = 56 \text{ m}^2$.

13. $\dfrac{6}{5}$: To find the surface area of a cube, find the area of 1 face, and multiply that by 6: $6(5^2) = 150$. To find the volume of a cube, cube its edge length: $5^3 = 125$.

The ratio of the cube's surface area to its volume, therefore, is $\dfrac{150}{125}$, or $\dfrac{6}{5}$.

14. **1 to 27:** First, let's call the length of one side of Cube A, x. Thus, the length of one side of Cube B is 3x. The volume of Cube A is x^3. The volume of Cube B is $(3x)^3$, or $27x^3$.

Therefore, the ratio of the volume of Cube A to Cube B is $\dfrac{x^3}{27x^3}$, or 1 to 27.

15. **3√2:** The area of the frame and the area of the picture sum to the total area of the image, which is 6^2, or 36. Therefore, the area of the frame and the picture are each equal to half of 36, or 18. Since EFGH is a square, the length of EF is $\sqrt{18}$, or $3\sqrt{2}$.

g

TRIANGLES & DIAGONALS

In This Chapter . . .

TRIANGLES & DIAGONALS

The most popular polygon on the GMAT is the triangle.

Right triangles (those with a 90° angle) require particular attention, because they have special properties that are useful for solving many GMAT geometry problems.

The most important property of a right triangle is the unique relationship of the three sides. Given the lengths of any two of the sides of a right triangle, one can determine the length of the third side using the Pythagorean Theorem. There are even two special types of right triangles—the 30-60-90 triangle and the 45-45-90 triangle—for which you only need the length of ONE side to determine the lengths of the triangle's other two sides.

Finally, right triangles are essential for solving problems involving other polygons. Cutting more complex polygons into right triangles is the MOST IMPORTANT TOOL for solving GMAT geometry problems.

The sum of the interior angles of a triangle is 180°.

The Angles of a Triangle

The angles in any given triangle have two key properties:

(1) The sum of the three angles of a triangle equals 180°.

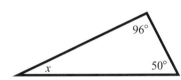

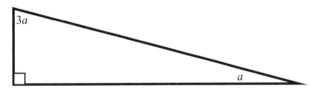

What is x? Since the sum of the three angles must be 180°, we can solve for x as follows: $180 - 96 - 50 = x = 34°$.

What is a? Since the sum of the three angles must be 180°, we can solve for x as follows: $90 + 3a + a = 180 \rightarrow a = 22.5°$.

(2) Angles correspond to their opposite sides. This means that the largest angle is opposite the longest side, while the smallest angle is opposite the shortest side. Additionally, if two sides are equal, their opposite angles are also equal.

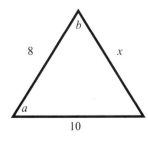

If angle a = angle b, what is the length of side x? As the opposite side of angle b has a length of 10, the opposite side of angle a must have the same length; therefore, $x = 10$.

The Sides of a Triangle

Consider the following "impossible" triangle and what it reveals about the relationship between the three sides of any triangle:

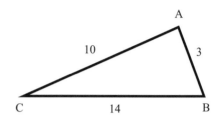

The triangle to the right could never be drawn with the given measurements. Why? Consider that the shortest distance between any two points is a straight line. According to the triangle shown, the direct straight line distance between point C and point B is 14; however, the indirect path from point C to B (the path that goes from C to A to B) is 10 + 3, or 13, which is shorter than the direct path! This is clearly impossible.

The sum of any two sides of a triangle must be GREATER than the third side. This is called the Triangle Inequality Theorem.

The above example leads to the following rule about the sides of any triangle:

> **The sum of any two sides of a triangle must be GREATER than the third side.**

Therefore, the maximum integer distance for side BC in the triangle above is 12. Alternatively, if side BC is in fact 14, then side AB must be at least 5, or side AC must be at least 12. Consider the following triangle and the proof that the given measurements are possible:

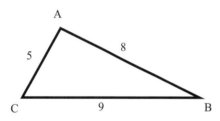

Test each combination of sides to prove that the measurements of this triangle are possible.

$$5 + 8 > 9$$
$$5 + 9 > 8$$
$$8 + 9 > 5$$

Note that the sum of two sides cannot be equal to the third side; the sum of two sides must always be GREATER than the third side.

The Pythagorean Theorem

A right triangle is a triangle with one right angle (90°). Every right triangle is composed of two legs and a hypotenuse. The hypotenuse is the side opposite the right angle and is often assigned the letter c. The two legs which form the right angle are often called a and b (it does not matter which leg is a and which leg is b).

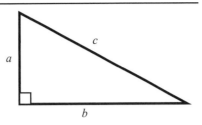

Given the lengths of two sides of a right triangle, how can you determine the length of the third side? Use the Pythagorean Theorem, which states that the sum of the square of the two legs of a right triangle $(a^2 + b^2)$ is equal to the square of the hypotenuse of that triangle (c^2).

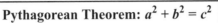

$$\boxed{\text{Pythagorean Theorem: } a^2 + b^2 = c^2}$$

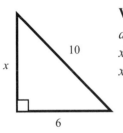

What is x?
$$a^2 + b^2 = c^2$$
$$x^2 + 6^2 = 10^2$$
$$x^2 + 36 = 100$$
$$x^2 = 64$$
$$x = 8$$

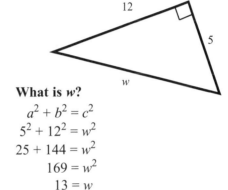

What is w?
$$a^2 + b^2 = c^2$$
$$5^2 + 12^2 = w^2$$
$$25 + 144 = w^2$$
$$169 = w^2$$
$$13 = w$$

Whenever you see a right triangle on the GMAT, look for a way to use the Pythagorean Theorem.

Common Right Triangles

Certain right triangles appear over and over on the GMAT. It pays to memorize these common combinations in order to save time on the exam. Instead of using the Pythagorean Theorem to solve for the lengths of the sides of these common right triangles, you should know the following Pythagorean triples from memory:

Common Combinations	Key Multiples
3 - 4 - 5 The most popular of all right triangles $3^2 + 4^2 = 5^2$ $(9 + 16 = 25)$	6 - 8 - 10 9 - 12 - 15 12 - 16 - 20
5 - 12 - 13 Also quite popular on the GMAT $5^2 + 12^2 = 13^2$ $(25 + 144 = 169)$	10 - 24 - 26
8 - 15 - 17 This one appears less frequently $8^2 + 15^2 = 17^2$ $(64 + 225 = 289)$	

*Manhattan*GMAT*Prep
the new standard

Isosceles Triangles and the 45 - 45 - 90 Triangle

An isosceles triangle is one in which two sides (and their corresponding angles) are equal. The most important isosceles triangle on the GMAT is the isosceles right triangle.

An isosceles right triangle has one 90° angle (opposite the hypotenuse) and two 45° angles (opposite the two equal legs). This triangle is called the 45 - 45 - 90 triangle.

The lengths of the legs of every 45 - 45 - 90 triangle have a specific ratio, which you must memorize:

45°	→ 45°	→ 90°
leg	leg	hypotenuse
1:	1:	$\sqrt{2}$

A 45 - 45 - 90 triangle is called an isosceles right triangle.

Given that side AB is 5, what are the lengths of sides BC and AC?

Since AB is 5, we use the ratio 1:1:$\sqrt{2}$ for sides AB: BC: AC to determine that the multiplier is 5. We then find that the sides of the triangle have lengths 5: 5: 5$\sqrt{2}$ (so side BC = 5 and side AC = 5$\sqrt{2}$).

Given that side AC is $\sqrt{18}$, what are the lengths of sides AB and BC?

Since AC is $\sqrt{18}$, we use the ratio 1:1:$\sqrt{2}$ for sides AB: BC: AC to determine that the multiplier is $\sqrt{18} \div \sqrt{2} = \sqrt{9} = 3$. We then find that the sides of the triangle have lengths 3: 3: 3$\sqrt{2}$ (so sides AB and BC are both equal to 3).

Why is the 45 - 45 - 90 triangle so important? Notice that this triangle is exactly half of a square! That is, two 45 - 45 - 90 triangles put together make up a square! Thus, if you are given the diagonal of a square, you can use the 45 - 45 - 90 ratio to find the length of a side of the square.

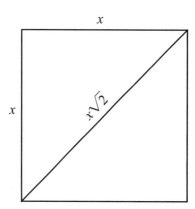

Equilateral Triangles and the 30 - 60 - 90 Triangle

An equilateral triangle is one in which all three sides (and all three angles) are equal. Each angle of an equilateral triangle is 60° (because all 3 angles must sum to 180°). A close relative of the equilateral triangle is the 30 - 60 - 90 triangle. Notice that two of these triangles put together from an equilateral triangle:

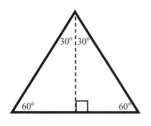

EQUILATERAL TRIANGLE

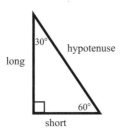

30 - 60 - 90 TRIANGLE

The lengths of the legs of every 30 - 60 - 90 triangle have the following ratio, which you must memorize:

30°	→	60°	→	90°
short leg		long leg		hypotenuse
1:		$\sqrt{3}$:		2

Remember, $\sqrt{3}$ corresponds to the long leg of the triangle, and 2 corresponds to the hypotenuse, which is actually the longest side. $\sqrt{3} < 2$

Given that the short leg of a 30 - 60 - 90 triangle has a length of 6, what are the lengths of the long leg and the hypotenuse?

The short leg, opposite the 30 degree angle, is 6, so we use the ratio 1:$\sqrt{3}$: 2 to determine that the multiplier is 6. We then find that the sides of the triangle have lengths 6: 6$\sqrt{3}$: 12 (so the long leg measures 6$\sqrt{3}$ and the hypotenuse measures 12).

Given that an equilateral triangle has a side length of 10, what is its height?

Looking at the equilateral triangle above, we can see that the side of an equilateral triangle is the same as the hypotenuse of a 30 - 60 - 90 triangle. Additionally, the height of an equilateral triangle is the same as the long leg of a 30 - 60 - 90 triangle. Since we are told that the hypotenuse is 10, we use the ratio 1:$\sqrt{3}$: 2 to determine that the multiplier is 5. We then find that the sides of the 30 - 60 - 90 triangle have lengths 5: 5$\sqrt{3}$: 10 (so the long leg = 5$\sqrt{3}$, which is the height of the equilateral triangle).

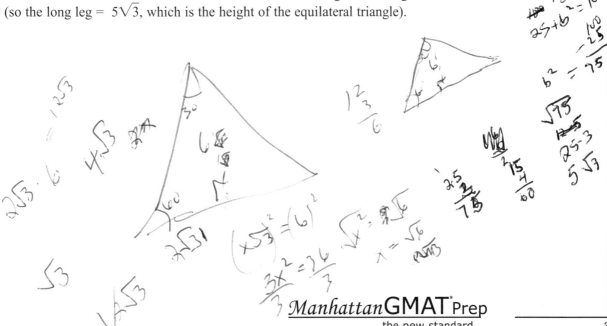

Manhattan **GMAT** Prep
the new standard

Diagonals of Other Polygons

Right triangles are useful for more than just triangles. They are also helpful for finding the diagonals of other polygons, specifically squares, cubes, rectangles, and rectangular solids.

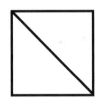

The diagonal of a square can be found using the formula:
$d = s\sqrt{2}$, where s is a side of the square.

The diagonal of a cube can be found using the formula:
$d = s\sqrt{3}$, where s is an edge of the cube.

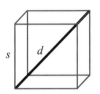

Recall that the diagonal of a square is the hypotenuse of a 45 - 45 - 90 triangle.

Given a square with side 5, what is the diagonal of the square?

Using the formula, $d = s\sqrt{2}$, we find that the diagonal of the square is $5\sqrt{2}$.

What is the measure of an edge of a cube with a diagonal of $\sqrt{60}$?

Again, using the formula, $d = s\sqrt{3}$, we solve as follows:

$$\sqrt{60} = s\sqrt{3} \rightarrow s = \frac{\sqrt{60}}{\sqrt{3}} = \sqrt{20}$$

Thus, the edge of the cube is $\sqrt{20}$.

To find the diagonal of a rectangle, you must know the length and the width, OR one dimension and the proportion of one to the other.

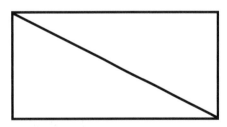

If the rectangle to the left has a length of 12 and a width of 5, what is the diagonal?

Using the Pythagorean Theorem, we solve:
$$5^2 + 12^2 = c^2 \rightarrow 25 + 144 = c^2 \rightarrow c = 13$$

The diagonal is 13.

If the rectangle above has a width of 6, and the ratio of the width to the length is 3:4, what is the diagonal?

Using the ratio, we find that the length is 8. Then, we can use the Pythagorean Theorem, or recognize that this is a 6-8-10 triangle, so the diagonal is 10.

What is the length of the diagonal of this rectangular solid?

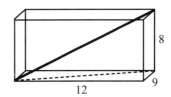

To find the diagonal of a rectangular solid, use the Pythagorean Theorem TWICE.

First, find the diagonal of the bottom face: $9^2 + 12^2 = c^2$ yields $c = 15$ (this is a multiple of a 3-4-5 triangle), so the bottom (dashed) diagonal is 15. Then, we can consider this bottom diagonal of length 15 as the base leg of another right triangle with a height of 8. Now we use the Pythagorean Theorem a second time: $8^2 + 15^2 = c^2$ yields $c = 17$, so the long diagonal is 17.

Similar Triangles

One final tool that you can use for GMAT triangle problems is the similar triangle strategy. Often, looking for similar triangles can help you solve complex problems.

Triangles are defined as similar if all their corresponding angles are equal and their corresponding sides are in proportion.

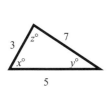 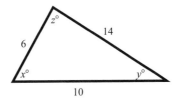

Once you find that triangles have 2 equal angles, you know they are similar. (If 2 angles are congruent, then the third angle must be congruent, since the sum of the angles in any triangle is 180°.)

What is the length of side EF?

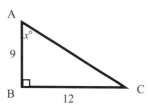 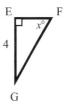

We know that the above two triangles are similar, because they have 2 angles in common (x and the right angle). Since they are similar triangles, their corresponding sides must be in proportion.

Side BC corresponds to side EG (since they both are opposite angle x). Since they are in the ratio of 12:4, we can determine that the large triangle is three times bigger than the smaller one, or in the ratio of 3:1. Using this ratio, we can determine that, since side AB corresponds to side EF, and AB is 9, side EF must be 3.

$$\frac{12}{4} = \frac{9}{x}$$

$$12x = 36$$

$$x = 3$$

If two right triangles have one other angle in common, they are similar triangles.

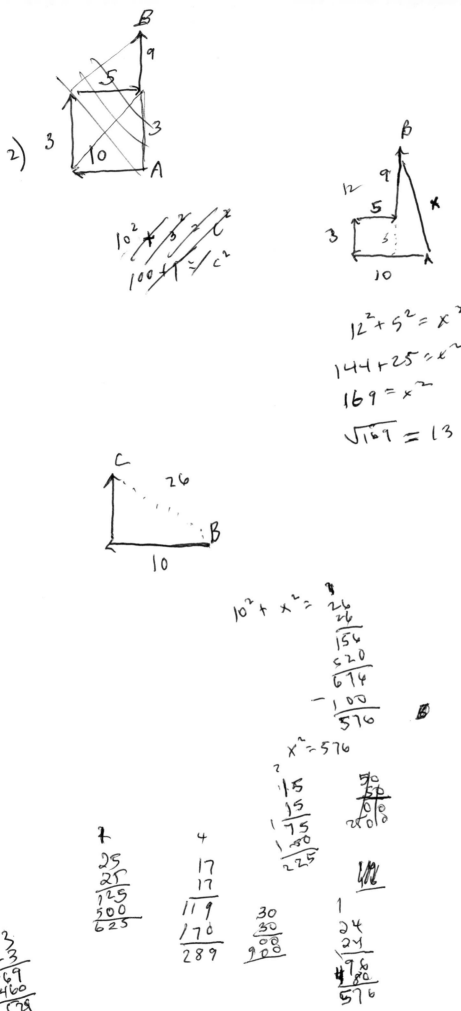

2)

B
9
5
3
3
10
A

$10^2 + 3^2 = C$
$100 + ? = C^2$

B
9
12
5
x
3
5
10
A

$12^2 + 5^2 = x^2$
$144 + 25 = x^2$
$169 = x^2$
$\sqrt{169} = 13$

C
26
B
10

$10^2 + x^2 = 26$

```
   26
   26
  156
  520
  674
 -100
  576    B
```

$x^2 = 576$

```
  15
  15
  75
 150
 225
```

```
 50
 50
 00
2500
```

7
```
 25
 25
125
500
625
```

4
```
 17
 17
119
170
289
```

```
 30
 30
 00
900
```

1
```
 24
 24
 96
480
576
```

```
 23
 23
 69
460
529
```

Problem Set (Note: Figures are not drawn to scale.)

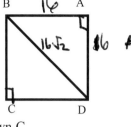

1. A square is bisected into two equal triangles (see figure). If BD is $16\sqrt{2}$ inches, what is the area of the square?

2. Beginning in Town A, Biker Bob rides his bike 10 miles west, 3 miles north, 5 miles east, and then 9 miles north, to Town B. How far apart are Town A and Town B?

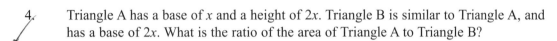

3. Now in Town B, Biker Bob goes due west, and then straight north to Town C. Town B and Town C are 26 miles apart. If Biker Bob went 10 miles west, how many miles north did he go?

4. Triangle A has a base of x and a height of $2x$. Triangle B is similar to Triangle A, and has a base of $2x$. What is the ratio of the area of Triangle A to Triangle B?

5. What is the measure of angle x in the figure to the right?

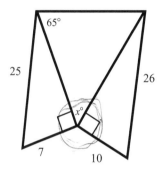

6. The longest side of an isosceles right triangle measures $20\sqrt{2}$. What is the area of the triangle?

7. Two similar triangles have areas in the ratio of 9:1. What is the ratio of these triangles' perimeters?

8. The size of a square computer screen is measured by the length of its diagonal. How much bigger is the visible area of a square 24-inch screen than the area of a square 20-inch screen?

9. A square field has an area of 400 square meters. Posts are set at all corners of the field. What is the longest distance between any two posts?

10. In Triangle ABC, AD = DB = DC (see figure). Given that angle DCB is 60° and angle ACD is 20°, what is angle x?

11. Two sides of a triangle are 4 and 10. If the third side is an integer x, how many possible values are there for x?

12. Jack makes himself a clay box in the shape of a cube, the edges of which are 4 inches long. What's the longest object he could fit inside the box (i.e., what is the diagonal of the cube)?

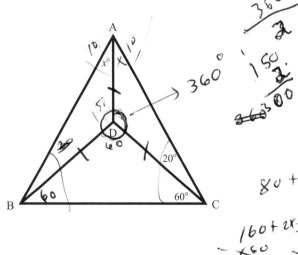

13. What is the area of an equilateral triangle whose sides measure 8 cm long?

14. Alexandra wants to pack away her posters without bending them. She rolls up the posters to put in a rectangular box that is 120 inches long, 90 inches wide, and 80 inches high. What is the longest a poster can be for Alexandra to pack it away without bending it (i.e., what is the diagonal of the rectangular box)?

15. The points of a six-pointed star consist of six identical equilateral triangles, with each side 4 cm (see figure). What is the area of the entire star, including the center?

1. **256 square units:** The diagonal of a square is $s\sqrt{2}$; therefore, the side length of square ABCD is 16. The area of the square is s^2, or $16^2 = 256$.

2. **13 miles:** If you draw a rough sketch of the path Biker Bob takes, as shown to the right, you can see that the direct distance from A to B forms the hypotenuse of a right triangle. The short leg (horizontal) is $10 - 5 = 5$ miles, and the long leg (vertical) is $9 + 3 = 12$ miles. Therefore, you can use the Pythagorean Theorem to find the direct distance from A to B:

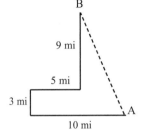

$$5^2 + 12^2 = c^2$$
$$25 + 144 = c^2$$
$$c^2 = 169$$
$$c = 13$$

You might recognize the common right triangle: 5 - 12 - 13.

3. **24 miles:** If you draw a rough sketch of the path Biker Bob takes, as shown to the right, you can see that the direct distance from B to C forms the hypotenuse of a right triangle.

$$10^2 + b^2 = 26^2$$
$$100 + b^2 = 676$$
$$b^2 = 576$$
$$b = 24$$

To find the square root of 576, you may find it helpful to prime factor it first:
$$576 = 2^6 \times 3^2$$
Therefore, $\sqrt{576} = 2^3 \times 3 = 24$.

You might recognize this as a multiple of the common 5 - 12 - 13 triangle.

4. **1 to 4:** Since we know that Triangle B is similar to Triangle A, we can set up a proportion to represent the relationship between the sides of both triangles:

$$\frac{\text{base}}{\text{height}} = \frac{x}{2x} = \frac{2x}{?}$$

By proportional reasoning, the height of Triangle B must be $4x$. Calculate the area of each triangle with the formula:

Triangle A: $A = \dfrac{b \times h}{2} = \dfrac{(x)(2x)}{2} = x^2$

Triangle B: $A = \dfrac{b \times h}{2} = \dfrac{(2x)(4x)}{2} = 4x^2$

The ratio of the area of Triangle A to Triangle B is 1 to 4.

5. **50°:** Use the Pythagorean Theorem to establish the missing lengths of the two right triangles on the right and left sides of the figure:

$$7^2 + b^2 = 25^2 \qquad\qquad 10^2 + b^2 = 26^2$$
$$49 + b^2 = 625 \qquad\qquad 100 + b^2 = 676$$
$$b^2 = 576 \qquad\qquad\quad b^2 = 576$$
$$b = 24 \qquad\qquad\qquad b = 24$$

The inner triangle is isosceles. Therefore, both angles opposite the equal sides measure 65°. Since there are 180° in a right triangle, $x = 180 - 2(65) = 50°$.

6. **200:** An isosceles right triangle is a 45 - 45 - 90 triangle, with sides in the ratio of 1:1:$\sqrt{2}$. If the longest side, the hypotenuse, measures $20\sqrt{2}$, the two other sides each measure 20. Therefore, the area of the triangle is:

$$A = \frac{b \times h}{2} = \frac{20 \times 20}{2} = 200$$

7. **3 to 1:** If two triangles have areas in the ratio of 9 to 1, their linear measurements have a ratio of $\sqrt{9}$ to $\sqrt{1}$, or 3 to 1. You can derive this rule algebraically with the following reasoning:

Imagine two similar triangles: a smaller one with base b and height h, and a larger one with base bx and height hx. The ratio of the areas of the larger triangle to the smaller one, therefore, would be:

$$\frac{.5(bx \times hx)}{.5(b \times h)} = \frac{.5bhx^2}{.5bh} = \frac{x^2}{1}$$ If we know that $x^2 = 9$, then $x = 3$. The ratio of the linear measurements (perimeter) is 3 to 1.

Alternately, solve this problem by picking real numbers. To do this, create two triangles whose areas have a 9:1 ratio.

First, draw the smaller triangle with an area of 6. Since the area of a triangle is half the product of the base and the height, the base and the height must multiply to 12. If possible, use a common right triangle: $3 \times 4 = 12$.

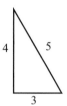

$$A_{\text{small}} = \frac{bh}{2} = \frac{3 \times 4}{2} = 6$$

Now draw the larger triangle. Since the smaller triangle has an area of 6, we need to draw a larger triangle with an area 9 times larger. $6 \times 9 = 54$. Since the area of a triangle is half the product of the base and height, the base and height must multiply to 108. If possible, use a common right triangle: $9 \times 12 = 108$.

$$A_{\text{large}} = \frac{bh}{2} = \frac{9 \times 12}{2} = 54$$

Then, find the ratio of the perimeters: $\dfrac{9 + 12 + 15}{3 + 4 + 5} = \dfrac{36}{12} = 3$.

8. **88 in²:** If the diagonal of the larger screen is 24 inches, and we know that $d = s\sqrt{2}$, then $s = \dfrac{24}{\sqrt{2}}$. By the same reasoning, the side length of the smaller screen is $\dfrac{20}{\sqrt{2}}$. The areas of the two screens are:

Large screen: $A = \dfrac{24}{\sqrt{2}} \times \dfrac{24}{\sqrt{2}} = 288$

Small screen: $A = \dfrac{20}{\sqrt{2}} \times \dfrac{20}{\sqrt{2}} = 200$

The visible area of the larger screen is 88 square inches bigger than the visible area of the smaller screen.

9: **20√2:** The longest distance between any two posts is the diagonal of the field. If the area of the field is 400 square meters, then each side must measure 20 meters. Diagonal = $d = s\sqrt{2}$, so $d = 20\sqrt{2}$.

10. **10:** If AD = DB = DC, then the three triangular regions in this figure are all isosceles triangles. Therefore, we can fill in some of the missing angle measurements as shown to the right. Since we know that there are 180° in the large triangle ABC, we can write the following equation:

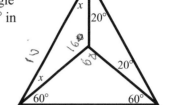

$$x + x + 20 + 20 + 60 + 60 = 180$$
$$2x + 160 = 180$$
$$x = 10$$

11. **7:** If two sides of a triangle are 4 and 10, the third side must be greater than $10 - 4$ and smaller than $10 + 4$. Therefore, the possible values for x are {7, 8, 9, 10, 11, 12, and 13}. You can draw a sketch to convince yourself of this:

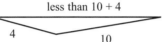

12. **4√3:** The diagonal of a cube is $s\sqrt{3}$. Therefore, the longest object Jack could fit inside the box would be $4\sqrt{3}$ inches long.

13. **16√3:** Draw in the height of the triangle (see figure). If triangle ABC is an equilateral triangle, and ABD is a right triangle, then ABD is a 30 - 60 - 90 triangle. Therefore, its sides are in the ratio of $1:\sqrt{3}:2$. If the hypotenuse is 8, the short leg is 4, and the long leg is $4\sqrt{3}$. This is the height of triangle ABC. Find the area of triangle ABC with the formula for area of a triangle:

$$A = \frac{b \times h}{2} = \frac{8 \times 4\sqrt{3}}{2} = 16\sqrt{3}$$

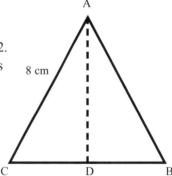

14. **170 inches:** Find the diagonal of this rectangular solid by applying the Pythagorean Theorem twice. First, find the diagonal across the bottom of the box:

$$120^2 + 90^2 = c^2$$
$$14,400 + 8100 = c^2$$

You might recognize this as a multiple of the common
3 - 4 - 5 right triangle.

$$c^2 = 22,500$$
$$c = 150$$

Then, find the diagonal of the rectangular box:

$$80^2 + 150^2 = c^2$$
$$6400 + 22,500 = c^2$$

You might recognize this as a multiple of the common
8 - 15 - 17 right triangle.

$$c^2 = 28,900$$
$$c = 170$$

15. **$48\sqrt{3}\,cm^2$:** We can think of this star as a large equilateral triangle with sides 12 cm long, and three additional smaller equilateral triangles with sides 4 inches long. Using the same 30 - 60 - 90 logic we applied in problem #13, we can see that the height of the larger equilateral triangle is $6\sqrt{3}$, and the height of the smaller equilateral triangle is $2\sqrt{3}$. Therefore, the areas of the triangles are as follows:

Large triangle: $\qquad A = \dfrac{b \times h}{2} = \dfrac{12 \times 6\sqrt{3}}{2} = 36\sqrt{3}$

Small triangles: $\qquad A = \dfrac{b \times h}{2} = \dfrac{4 \times 2\sqrt{3}}{2} = 4\sqrt{3}$

The total area of three smaller triangles and one large triangle is:
$$36\sqrt{3} + 3(4\sqrt{3}) = 48\sqrt{3}\,cm^2.$$

g

Chapter 3
of
GEOMETRY

CIRCLES &
CYLINDERS

In This Chapter . . .

CIRCLES & CYLINDERS

A circle is defined as the set of connected points in a plane that are equidistant from a fixed center point. A circle contains 360°.

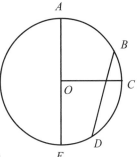

Any line segment that connects the center point to a point on the circle is termed a radius of the circle. Segment *OC* is the radius of the circle to the right.

Any line segment that connects two points on a circle is called a chord. Any chord that passes through the center of the circle is called a diameter. Notice that the diameter is two times the length of the radius. Line segment *BD* is a chord of the circle to the right. Line segment *AE* is a diameter of the circle.

The GMAT tests your ability to find (1) the circumference and (2) the area of whole and partial circles. In addition, you must know how to work with cylinders, a three-dimensional shape made, in part, of circles. The GMAT tests your ability to find (3) the surface area and (4) the volume of cylinders.

If you know the circumference, the radius, the diameter, or the area of a circle, you can use one to find any of the other measurements.

Circumference of a Circle

The distance around a circle is termed the circumference. This is equivalent to the perimeter of a polygon. The only information you need to find the circumference of a circle is the radius of that circle. The formula for the circumference of any circle is:

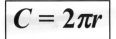

where *C* is the circumference, *r* is the radius, and π is a number that is approximately 3.14.

For the purposes of the GMAT, π should be approximated as 3. In fact, most problems require no approximation, as the GMAT includes π as part of the answer choices. For example, a typical answer choice for a circumference problem would be 8π, instead of 24.

What is the distance around a circle that has a diameter of 10?

To solve this, first determine the radius, which is half of the diameter, or 5. Then plug this into the circumference formula $C = 2\pi r = 2\pi(5) = 10\pi$. This is generally a sufficient answer. You do not need to multiply 10 by π.

$C = 2\pi r$

$C = 2\pi 5 = 10\pi$

Circumference and Arc Length

Often, the GMAT will ask you to solve for a portion of the distance on a circle, instead of the entire circumference. This portion is termed an arc. Arc length can be found by determining what fraction the arc is of the entire circumference. This can be done by looking at the central angle that defines the arc.

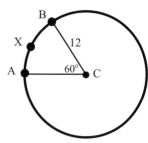

What is the length of arc AXB?

Arc AXB is the arc from A to B, passing through the point X. To find its length, first find the circumference of the circle. The radius is given as 12. To find the circumference, use the formula $C = 2\pi r = 2\pi(12) = 24\pi$.

Then, use the central angle to determine what fraction the arc is of the entire circle. Since the arc is defined by the central angle of 60 degrees, and the entire circle is 360 degrees, then the arc is $\dfrac{60}{360} = \dfrac{1}{6}$ of the circle.

Therefore, the measure of arc AXB $= \left(\dfrac{1}{6}\right)(24\pi) = 4\pi$.

Perimeter of a Sector

The boundaries of a sector of a circle are formed by the arc and two radii. Therefore, if you know the length of the radius and the central (or inscribed) angle, you can find the perimeter of the sector.

What is the perimeter of sector ABC?

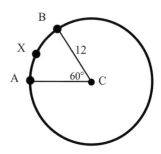

In the previous example, we found the length of arc AXB to be 4π. Therefore, the perimeter of the sector is:

$$4\pi + 12 + 12 = 24 + 4\pi.$$

There are a total of 360° in a circle.

Area of a Circle

The space inside a circle is termed the area of the circle. This is just like the area of a polygon. Just as with circumference, the only information you need to find the area of a circle is the radius of that circle. The formula for the area of any circle is:

$$A = \pi r^2$$

where A is the area, r is the radius, and π is a number that is approximately 3.14.

What is the area of a circle with a circumference of 16π?

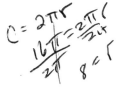

In order to find the area of a circle, all we must know is its radius. If the circumference of the circle is 16π (and $C = 2\pi r$), then the radius must be 8. Plug this into the area formula:

$$A = \pi r^2 = \pi(8^2) = 64\pi.$$

Central or inscribed angles can help you determine arc length and sector area.

Area of a Sector

Often, the GMAT will ask you to solve for the area of a portion of a circle, instead of the area of the entire circle. A portion of a circle is termed a sector. Sector area can be found by determining what fraction it is of the entire area. This can be done by looking at the central angle which defines the sector.

What is the area of sector ACB (the striped region) below?

First, find the area of the entire circle:
$$A = \pi r^2 = \pi(3^2) = 9\pi.$$

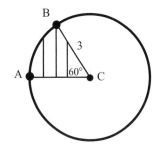

Then, use the central angle to determine what fraction the sector is of the entire circle. Since the sector is defined by the central angle of 60°, and the entire circle is 360°, the sector is a sixth of the area of the circle.

Therefore, the area of sector ACB is $\left(\dfrac{1}{6}\right)(9\pi) = 1.5\pi.$

Inscribed vs. Central Angles

Thus far, in dealing with arcs and sectors, we have referred to the concept of a central angle. A central angle is defined as an angle whose vertex lies at the center point of a circle. As we have seen, a central angle defines both an arc and a sector of a circle.

Another type of angle is termed an inscribed angle. An inscribed angle has its vertex on the circle itself. The following diagrams illustrate the difference between a central angle and an inscribed angle.

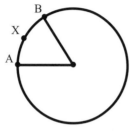

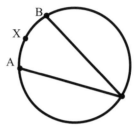

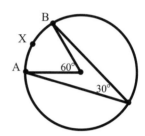

CENTRAL ANGLE   INSCRIBED ANGLE

Notice that, in the circle at the far right, there is a central angle and an inscribed angle, both of which intercept arc *AXB*. It is the central angle that defines the arc; that is, the arc is 60° (or one sixth of the complete 360° circle). An inscribed angle is equal to half of the arc it intercepts (in this case, the inscribed angle is 30°, which is half of 60°).

Inscribed Triangles

Related to this idea of an inscribed angle is that of an inscribed triangle. The important rule to remember is: **if a triangle is inscribed in a circle, such that one of its sides is a diameter of the circle, then the triangle MUST be a right triangle.** Conversely, any right triangle inscribed in a circle must have one of its sides as the diameter of the circle (thereby splitting the circle in half).

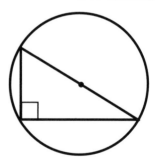

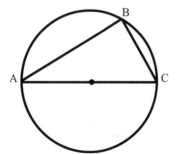

In the inscribed triangle to the left, triangle ABC must be a right triangle, since AC is a diameter of the circle.

*Manhattan*GMAT·Prep
the new standard

Sidebar:

If you are given the measure of an inscribed angle, find the measure of the corresponding central angle to solve the problem.

Cylinders and Surface Area

Two circles and a rectangle combine to form a three-dimensional shape called a right circular cylinder (referred to from now on simply as a cylinder). The top and bottom of the cylinder are circles, while the middle of the cylinder is formed from a rolled-up rectangle, as shown in the diagram below:

In order to determine the surface area of a cylinder, sum the areas of the 3 surfaces: The area of each circle is πr^2, while the area of the rectangle is length × width. Looking at the figures on the left, we can see that the length of the rectangle is equal to the circumference of the circle ($2\pi r$), and the width of the rectangle is equal to the height of the cylinder (h). Therefore, the area of the rectangle is $2\pi r$ × h. To find the total surface area of a cylinder, sum the surface area of the circular top and bottom, as well as the rectangle that wraps around the outside.

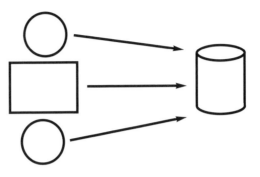

Think of the formula for the volume of a cylinder as the area of the circular base multiplied by the height, just like the formula for the volume of a rectangular solid.

$$SA = \textbf{2 circles} + \textbf{rectangle} = \textbf{2}(\pi r^2) + \textbf{2}\pi rh$$

The only information you need to find the surface area of a cylinder is (1) the radius of the cylinder and (2) the height of the cylinder.

Cylinders and Volume

The volume of a cylinder measures how much "stuff" it can hold inside. In order to find the volume of a cylinder, use the following formula:

$$V = \pi r^2 h$$

where V is the volume, r is the radius of the cylinder, and h is the height of the cylinder.

As with finding surface area, determining the volume of a cylinder requires two pieces of information: (1) the radius of the cylinder and (2) the height of the cylinder.

The diagram below shows that two cylinders can have the same volume but different shapes (and therefore each fits differently inside a larger object).

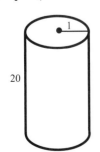

$$V = \pi r^2 h$$
$$= \pi(1)^2 20$$
$$= 20\pi$$

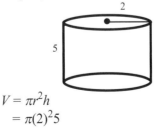

$$V = \pi r^2 h$$
$$= \pi(2)^2 5$$
$$= 20\pi$$

Problem Set (Note: Figures are not drawn to scale.)

1. Triangle ABC is inscribed in a circle, such that AC is a diameter of the circle (see figure). If AB is 8 and BC is 15, what is the circumference of the circle?

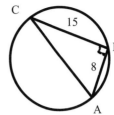

2. A cylinder has a surface area of 360π, and is 3 units tall. What is the diameter of the cylinder's circular base?

3. Randy can run π meters every 20 seconds. If the circular track has a radius of 75 meters, how long does it take Randy to run twice around the track?

4. Randy then moves on to the Jumbo Track, which has a radius of 200 meters (as compared to the first track, with a radius of 75 meters). Ordinarily, Randy runs 8 laps on the normal track.   How many laps on the Jumbo Track would Randy have to run in order to have the same workout?

5. A circular lawn with a radius of 5 meters is surrounded by a circular walkway that is 4 meters wide (see figure). What is the area of the walkway?

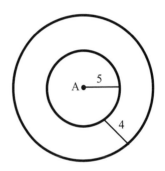

6. A cylindrical water tank has a diameter of 14 meters and a height of 20 meters. A water truck can fill π cubic meters of the tank every minute. How long will it take the water truck to fill the water tank from empty to half-full?

7. Red Giant cola comes in two sizes, Giant and Super-Giant. Each comes in a cylindrical container, and the Giant size sells for $1.20. If the Super-Giant container has twice the height and its circular base has twice the radius of the Giant size, and the price per ml of Red Giant cola is the same, how much does the Super-Giant container cost?

8. BE and CD are both diameters of Circle A (see figure). If the area of Circle A is 180 units^2, what is the area of sector ABC + sector ADE?

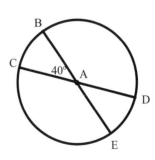

9. Jane has to paint a cylindrical column that is 14 feet high and that has a circular base with a radius of 3 feet. If one bucket of paint will cover 10π square feet, how many buckets does Jane need to buy in order to paint the column, including the top and bottom?

10. A rectangular box has the dimensions 12 inches $\times$ 10 inches $\times$ 8 inches. What is the largest possible volume of a right cylinder that is placed inside the box?

11. A circular flower bed takes up half the area of a square lawn. If an edge of the lawn is 200 feet long, what is the radius of the flower bed? (Express the answer in terms of π .)

12.   If angle ABC is 40 degrees (see figure), and the area of the circle is 81π, how long is arc AXC?

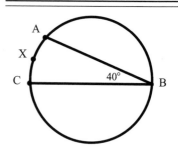

13.   A Hydrogenator water gun has a cylindrical water tank, which is 30 centimeters long. Jack fills his Hydrogenator at a hose that will fill up π cubic centimeters of his water tank every second. If it takes him 8 minutes to fill the tank with water, what is the diameter of the circular base of the gun's water tank?

14.   Triangle ABC is inscribed in a circle, such that AC is a diameter of the circle and angle BAC is 45° (see figure). If the area of Triangle ABC is 72 square units, how much larger is the area of the circle than the area of Triangle ABC?

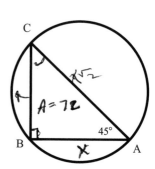

15.   Triangle ABC is inscribed in a circle, such that AC is a diameter of the circle and angle BAC is 45°. (Refer to the same figure as for problem #14.) If the area of Triangle ABC is 84.5 square units, what is the length of arc BC?

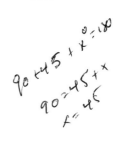

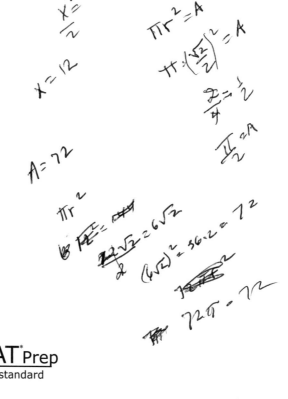

1. **17π:** If AC is a diameter of the circle, then inscribed triangle ABC is a right triangle, with AC as the hypotenuse. Therefore, we can apply the Pythagorean Theorem to find the length of AC.

$8^2 + 15^2 = c^2$

$64 + 225 = c^2$ The circumference of the circle is $2\pi r$, or 17π.

$c^2 = 289$

$c = 17$ You might recognize the common 8 -15 - 17 right triangle.

2. **24:** The surface area of a cylinder is the area of the circular top and bottom, plus the area of its wrapped-around rectangular third face. We can express this in formula form as:

$SA = 2(\pi r^2) + 2\pi rh$

Substitute the known values into this formula to find the radius of the circular base:

$360\pi = 2(\pi r^2) + 2\pi r(3)$

$360\pi = 2\pi r^2 + 6\pi r$

$r^2 + 3r - 180 = 0$

$(r + 15)(r - 12) = 0$

$r + 15 = 0$ OR $r - 12 = 0$

$r = \{-15, 12\}$

Use only the positive value of r: 12. If $r = 12$, the diameter of the cylinder's circular base is 24.

3. **1 hour and 40 minutes:** The distance around the track is the circumference of the circle:

$C = 2\pi r$

$\quad = 150\pi$

Running twice around the circle would equal a distance of 300π meters. If Randy can run π meters every 20 seconds, he runs 3π meters every minute. Therefore, it will take him 100 minutes (or 1 hour and 40 minutes) to run around the circular track twice.

4. **3 laps:** 8 laps on the normal track is a distance of 1200π meters. (Recall from problem #3 that the circumference of the normal track is 150π meters.) If the Jumbo Track has a radius of 200 meters, its circumference is 400π meters. It will take 3 laps around this track to travel 1200π meters.

5. **$56\pi\text{m}^2$:** The area of the walkway is the area of the entire image (walkway + lawn) minus the area of the lawn. To find the area of each circle, use the formula:

Large circle: $A = \pi r^2 = \pi(9)^2 = 81\pi$

Small circle: $A = \pi r^2 = \pi(5)^2 = 25\pi$ $81\pi - 25\pi = 56\pi\text{m}^2$

6. **8 hours and 10 minutes:** First find the volume of the cylindrical tank:

$V = \pi r^2 \times h$

$\quad = \pi(7)^2 \times 20$

$\quad = 980\pi$

If the water truck can fill π cubic meters of the tank every minute, it will take 980 minutes to fill the tank completely; therefore, it will take $980 \div 2 = 490$ minutes to fill the tank halfway. This is equal to 8 hours and 10 minutes.

7. **$9.60:** Let h = the height of the giant size → $2h$ = the height of the super-giant size.
Let r = the radius of the giant size → $2r$ = the radius of the super-giant size.

The volume of the giant can = $\pi r^2 h$.
The volume of the super-giant can = $\pi(2r)^2 \times 2h = 8(\pi r^2 \times h) = 8\pi r^2 h$.
The super-giant can holds 8 times as much cola. If the price per ml is the same, and the Giant can sells for $1.20, the Super-Giant can sells for 8($1.20) = $9.60.

8. **40 units^2:** The two central angles, CAB and DAE, describe a total of 80°. Simplify the fraction to find out what fraction of the circle this represents:

$$\frac{80}{360} = \frac{2}{9} \qquad \frac{2}{9} \text{ of } 180 \text{ units}^2 \text{ is } 40 \text{ units}^2.$$

9. **11 buckets:** The surface area of a cylinder is the area of the circular top and bottom, plus the area of its wrapped-around rectangular third face.

Top & Bottom: $A = \pi r^2 = 9\pi$
Rectangle: $A = 2\pi r \times h = 84\pi$

The total surface area, then, is $9\pi + 9\pi + 84\pi = 102\pi$ ft^2. If one bucket of paint will cover 10π ft^2, then Jane will need 10.2 buckets to paint the entire column. Since paint stores do not sell fractional buckets, she will need to purchase 11 buckets.

10. **200π:** The radius of the cylinder must be equal to half of the smaller of the 2 dimensions that form the box's bottom. The height, then, can be equal to the remaining dimension of the box. Since the radius is squared in the formula, it is essentially counted twice, while the height is only counted once. Thus, the largest possible radius will result in the cylinder with the largest volume. Therefore, a radius of 5 (half of 10, the smaller of the box's 10 x 12 bottom dimensions) and a height of 8 will result in the largest possible volume:

$$V = \pi r^2 \times h$$
$$= 25\pi \times 8 = 200\pi$$

11. $\sqrt{\dfrac{20,000}{\pi}}$: The area of the lawn is $(200)^2 = 40,000$ ft^2.

Therefore, the area of the flower bed is $40,000 \div 2 = 20,000$ ft^2.

$A = \pi r^2 = 20,000$ The radius of the flower bed is equal to $\sqrt{\dfrac{20,000}{\pi}}$.

12. **4π:** If the area of the circle is 81π, then the radius of the circle is 9 ($A = \pi r^2$). Therefore, the total circumference of the circle is 18π ($C = 2\pi r$). Angle ABC, an inscribed angle of 40°, corresponds to a central angle of 80°. Thus, arc AXC is equal to 80/360 = 2/9 of the total circumference:
$$2/9(18\pi) = 4\pi.$$

13. **8 cm:** In 8 minutes, or 480 seconds, 480 πcm^3 of water flows into the tank. Therefore, the volume of the tank is 480π. We are given a height of 30, so we can solve for the radius.

$$V = \pi r^2 \times h$$
$$480\pi = 30\pi r^2$$
$$r^2 = 16$$
$$r = 4$$

Therefore, the diameter of the tank's base is 8 cm.

14. **72π − 72:** If AC is a diameter of the circle, then angle ABC is a right angle. Therefore, triangle ABC is a 45 - 45 - 90 triangle, and the base and height are equal. Assign the variable x to represent both the base and height:

$$A = \frac{bh}{2} \qquad\qquad \frac{x^2}{2} = 72$$
$$x^2 = 144$$
$$x = 12$$

The base and height of the triangle are equal to 12, and so the area of the triangle is $\frac{12 \times 12}{2} = 72$.

The hypotenuse of the triangle, which is also the diameter of the circle, is equal to $12\sqrt{2}$. Therefore, the radius is equal to $6\sqrt{2}$ and the area of the circle, πr^2, = 72π. The area of the circle is $72\pi - 72$ square units larger than the area of triangle ABC.

15. $\frac{13\sqrt{2}\pi}{4}$: We know that the area of triangle ABC is 84.5 square units, so we can use the same logic as in the previous problem to establish the base and height of the triangle:

$$A = \frac{bh}{2} \qquad\qquad \frac{x^2}{2} = 84.5$$
$$x^2 = 169$$
$$x = 13$$

The base and height of the triangle are equal to 13. Therefore, the hypotenuse, which is also the diameter of the circle, is equal to $13\sqrt{2}$, and the circumference ($C = \pi d$) is equal to $13\sqrt{2}\pi$. Angle A, an inscribed angle, corresponds to a central angle of 90°. Thus, arc BC = 90/360 = 1/4 of the total circumference:

$$\frac{1}{4} \text{ of } 13\sqrt{2}\pi \text{ is } \frac{13\sqrt{2}\pi}{4}.$$

g

Chapter 4
of

GEOMETRY

LINES &
ANGLES

In This Chapter . . .

- Intersecting Lines
- Exterior Angles of a Triangle
- Parallel Lines Cut by a Transversal

LINES & ANGLES

A straight line is 180°. Think of a line as half of a circle.

Parallel lines are lines in a plane that never intersect. No matter how far you extend the lines, they never meet. Two parallel lines are shown below:

Perpendicular lines are lines that intersect at a 90° angle. Two perpendicular lines are shown below:

There are two major line-angle relationships that you must know for the GMAT:
  (1) The angles formed by any intersecting lines.
  (2) The angles formed by parallel lines cut by a transversal.

Intersecting Lines

Intersecting lines have three important properties.

First, the interior angles formed by intersecting lines form a circle, so the sum of these angles is 360°. In the diagram shown, $a + b + c + d = 360$.

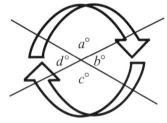

Second, interior angles that combine to form a line sum to 180°. These are termed supplementary angles. Thus, in the diagram shown, $a + b = 180$, because angles a and b form a line together. Other supplementary angles are: $b + c = 180$, $c + d = 180$, and $d + a = 180$.

Third, angles formed by the same two lines are equal. These are called vertical angles. Thus, in the diagram above, $a = c$, because both of these angles are formed from the same two lines. Additionally, $b = d$ for the same reason.

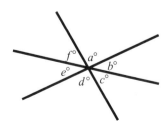

Note that all of the above rules apply to more than two lines that intersect at a point, as shown to the left. In the diagram to the left, $a + b + c + d + e + f = 360$, because these angles combine to form a circle. In addition, $a + b + c = 180$, because these three angles combine to form a line. Finally, $a = d$, $b = e$, and $c = f$, because these are pairs of vertical angles.

*Manhattan*GMAT*Prep

Exterior Angles of a Triangle

An exterior angle of a triangle is equal in measure to the sum of the two non-adjacent interior angles of the triangle.

$a + b + c = 180$ (sum of angles in a triangle).
$b + x = 180$ (supplementary angles).
Therefore, $x = a + c$.

Sometimes parallel lines cut by a transversal appear when a rectangle, a parallelogram, a rhombus, or a trapezoid is cut in half by a diagonal.

Parallel Lines Cut By a Transversal

The GMAT makes frequent use of diagrams that include parallel lines cut by a transversal, as shown here.

Notice that there are 8 angles formed by this construction, but there are only TWO different angle measures (*a* and *b*). All the acute angles formed when parallel lines are cut by a transversal are congruent. Likewise, all the obtuse angles formed are congruent. Any acute angle is supplementary to any obtuse angle. Thus, any *a* summed with any *b* will yield 180.

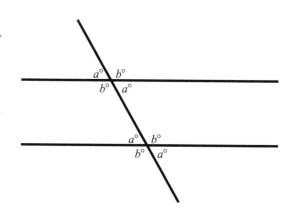

Whenever you see a transversal problem on the GMAT, immediately fill in all the *a* (acute) and *b* (obtuse) angles, just as in the diagram above. You will then be able to see all the angles that are equal, and all the combinations of angles that sum to 180°. This generally will lead you towards the solution to the problem.

Sometimes the GMAT disguises the parallel lines and the transversal so that they are not readily apparent, as in the diagram pictured to the right.

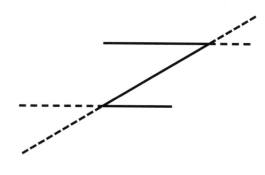

In these "disguised" cases, it is a good idea to extend the lines so that you can easily see the parallel lines and the transversal. Just remember always to be on the lookout for parallel lines; when you see them, start extending lines and labeling the acute and obtuse angles.

Problem Set

Problems 1 through 4 refer to the diagram below, where line AB is parallel to line CD.

1.   If $x - y = 10$, what is x?   *95*

2.   If the ratio of x to y is 3:2, what is y?

3.   If $x + (x + y) = 320$, what is x?

4.   If $\dfrac{x}{x - y} = 2$, what is x?

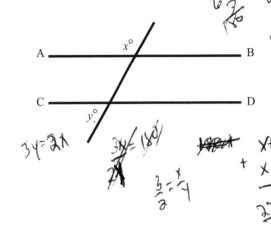

Problems 5 through 8 refer to the diagram below.

5.   If a is 95, what is $b + d - e$?   *95*

6.   If $c + f = 70$, and d is 80, what is b?

7.   If $a + b$ are complementary angles (they sum to 90°), name three other pairs of complementary angles.

8.   If e is 45, what is the sum of all the other angles?

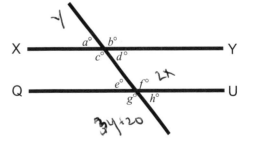

Problems 9 through 12 refer to the diagram below, where line XY is parallel to line QU.

9.   If $a + e = 150$, find f.

10.   If $a = y$, $g = 3y + 20$, and $f = 2x$, find x.

11.   If $g = 11y$, $a = 4x - y$, and $d = 5y + 2x - 20$, find h.

12.   If $b = 4x$, $e = x + 2y$, and $d = 3y + 8$, find h.

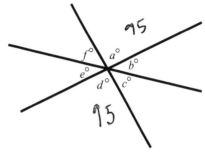

Problems 13 through 15 refer to the diagram to the right.

13.   If $c + g = 140$, find k.

14.   If $g = 90$, what is $a + k$?

15.   If $f + k = 150$, find b.

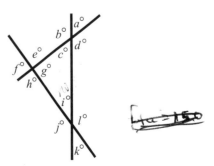

1. **95:** We know that $x + y = 180$, since any acute angle formed by a transversal that cuts across two parallel lines is supplementary to any obtuse angle. Use the information given to set up a system of two equations with two variables:

$$x + y = 180$$
$$\underline{x - y = \ 10}$$
$$2x = 190$$
$$x = 95$$

2. **72:** Set up a ratio, using the unknown multiplier, a.

$$\frac{x}{y} = \frac{3a}{2a}$$

$$180 = x + y = 3a + 2a = 5a$$
$$180 = 5a$$
$$a = 36$$
$$y = 2a = 2(36) = 72$$

3. **140:** Use the fact that $x + y = 180$ to set up a system of two equations with two variables:

$$x + y = 180 \quad \rightarrow \quad -x - y = -180$$
$$\underline{+ \quad 2x + y = \quad 320}$$
$$x \qquad = \quad 140$$

4. **120:** Use the fact that $x + y = 180$ to set up a system of two equations with two variables:

$$\frac{x}{x - y} = 2 \quad \rightarrow \quad x - 2y = 0$$
$$\underline{- \quad x + \ y = 180}$$
$$-3y = -180$$
$$y = 60 \quad \rightarrow \quad \text{Therefore, } x = 120.$$

5. **95:** Because a and d are vertical angles, they have the same measure: $a = d = 95°$. Likewise, since b and e are vertical angles, they have the same measure: $b = e$. Therefore, $b + d - e = d = 95°$.

6. **65:** Because c and f are vertical angles, they have the same measure: $c + f = 70$, so $c = f = 35$. Notice that b, c, and d form a straight line: $b + c + d = 180$. Substitute the known values of c and d into this equation:

$$b + 35 + 80 = 180$$
$$b + 115 = 180$$
$$b = 65$$

7. ***b* and *d*, *a* and *e*, & *d* and *e*:** If a is complementary to b, then d (which is equal to a, since they are vertical angles), is also complementary to b. Likewise, if a is complementary to b, then a is also complementary to e (which is equal to b, since they are vertical angles). Finally, d and e must be complementary, since $d = a$ and $e = b$.

8. **315:** If $e = 45°$, then the sum of all the other angles is $360 - 45 = 315$.

9. **105:** We are told that $a + e = 150$. Since they are both acute angles formed by a transversal cutting across two parallel lines, they are also congruent. Therefore, $a = e = 75$. Any acute angle in this diagram is supplementary to any obtuse angle, so $75 + f = 180$, and $f = 105$.

10. **70:** We know that angles a and g are supplementary; their measures sum to 180. Therefore:

$y + 3y + 20 = 180$

$4y = 160$ Angle f is congruent to angle g, so its measure is also $3y + 20$.

$y = 40$ The measure of angle $f = g = 3(40) + 20 = 140$. If $f = 2x$, then $140 = 2x \rightarrow x = 70$.

11. **70:** We are given the measure of one acute angle (a) and one obtuse angle (g). Since any acute angle in this diagram is supplementary to any obtuse angle, $11y + 4x - y = 180$, or $4x + 10y = 180$. Since angle d is congruent to angle a, we know that $5y + 2x - 20 = 4x - y$, or $2x - 6y = -20$. We can set up a system of two equations with two variables:

$$2x - 6y = -20 \qquad \rightarrow \qquad \begin{array}{r} -4x + 12y = 40 \\ \underline{4x + 10y = 180} \\ 22y = 220 \\ y = 10; x = 20 \end{array}$$

Since h is one of the acute angles, h has the same measure as a: $4x - y = 4(20) - 10 = 70$.

12. **68:** Because b and d are supplementary, $4x + 3y + 8 = 180$, or $4x + 3y = 172$. Since d and e are congruent, $3y + 8 = x + 2y$, or $x - y = 8$. We can set up a system of two equations with two variables:

$$x - y = 8 \qquad \rightarrow \qquad \begin{array}{r} 4x + 3y = 172 \\ \underline{3x - 3y = 24} \\ 7x = 196 \\ x = 28; y = 20 \end{array}$$

Since h is congruent to d, $h = 3y + 8$, or $3(20) + 8 = 68$.

13. **40:** If $c + g = 140$, then $i = 40$, because there are $180°$ in a triangle. Since k is vertical to i, k is also $= 40$. Alternately, if $c + g = 140$, then $j = 140$, since j is an exterior angle of the triangle and is therefore equal to the sum of the two remote interior angles. Since k is supplementary to j, $k = 180 - 140 = 40$.

14. **90:** If $g = 90$, then the other two angles in the triangle, c and i, sum to 90. Since a and k are vertical angles to c and i, they sum to 90 as well.

15. **150:** Angles f and k are vertical to angles g and i. These two angles, then, must also sum to 150. Angle b, an exterior angle of the triangle, must be equal to the sum of the two remote interior angles g and i. Therefore, $b = 150$.

g

of

Chapter 5

GEOMETRY

COORDINATE
PLANE

In This Chapter . . .

- The Slope of a Line
- The 4 Types of Slopes
- The Intercepts of a Line
- Slope-Intercept Equation
- Horizontal and Vertical Lines
- Step by Step: From 2 Points to a Line
- The Distance Between 2 Points
- Positive and Negative Quadrants
- Perpendicular Bisectors

THE COORDINATE PLANE

The coordinate plane is formed by a horizontal axis (the "*x*" axis) and a vertical axis (the "*y*" axis), as shown here.

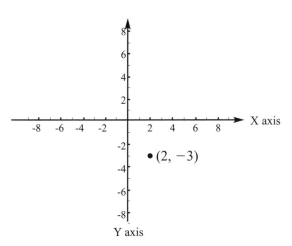

The purpose of the coordinate plane is to help us identify points. Points are identified by using an ordered pair, such as the one to the left $(2, -3)$. The first member of the ordered pair (2) is the *x*-coordinate, and corresponds to the point's location on the horizontal axis. The second member of the ordered pair is the *y*-coordinate, and corresponds to the point's location on the vertical axis. A line in the plane is formed by the connection of two or more points. The GMAT tests your ability to use ordered pairs and lines in the coordinate plane.

The slope of a line is equal to
$$\frac{\text{rise}}{\text{run}} = \frac{y_1 - y_2}{x_1 - x_2}$$

$$\frac{y_1 - y_2}{x_1 - x_2} = slope$$

The Slope of a Line

The slope of a line is defined as the rise over the run—that is, the amount the line rises vertically over the amount the line runs horizontally.

The slope of a line can be determined by taking two points on the line and determining the difference between their *x*-coordinates and their *y*-coordinates.

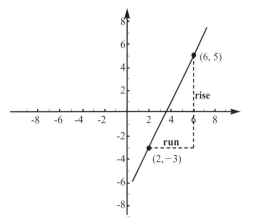

The line rises vertically from -3 to 5. This distance can be found by subtracting the *y*-coordinates: $5 - (-3) = 8$. Thus, the line rises 8 units.

The line runs horizontally from 2 to 6. This distance can be found by subtracting the *x*-coordinates: $6 - 2 = 4$. Thus, the line runs 4 units.

Therefore, the slope of the line is: $\dfrac{\text{rise}}{\text{run}} = \dfrac{8}{4} = 2$.

The 4 Types of Slopes

There are four types of slopes that a line can have:

Think of slope as walking from left to right. If you walked along a line with a positive slope, you would walk *up*.

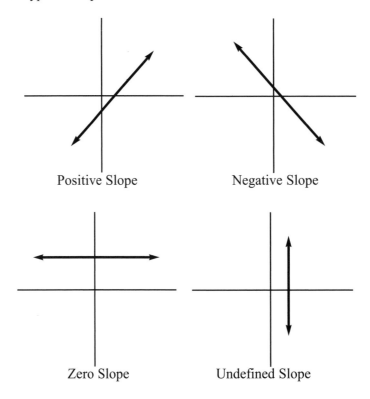

Positive Slope   Negative Slope

Zero Slope   Undefined Slope

A positive slope rises upward from left to right. A negative slope falls downward from left to right. A zero slope is a horizontal line. An undefined slope is a vertical line, also called "no slope."

The Intercepts of a Line

The point where a line hits the coordinate axis is called the intercept. There are two types of intercepts: the *y*-intercept, where the line hits the *y*-axis, and the *x*-intercept, where the line hits the *x*-axis.

The *y*-intercept is expressed using the ordered pair (0, *y*), where *y* is the point that the line hits the *y*-axis. In the diagram to the right, 6 is the *y*-intercept, expressed by the ordered pair (0,6).

The *x*-intercept is expressed using the ordered pair (*x*, 0), where *x* is the point that the line hits the *x*-axis. In the diagram to the right, the *x*-intercept is −4, and is expressed by the ordered pair (−4, 0).

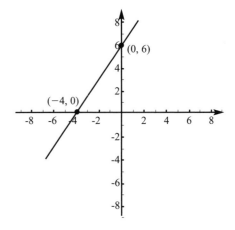

Slope-Intercept Equation: $y = mx + b$

All lines can be written as equations in the form $y = mx + b$, where m represents the slope of the line and b represents the y-intercept of the line. Some examples:

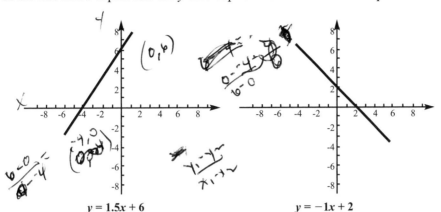

$y = 1.5x + 6$	$y = -1x + 2$
The slope of the line is 1.5 (positive).	The slope of the line is -1 (negative).
The y-intercept of the line is 6.	The y-intercept of the line is 2.

Vertical lines take the form $x = $ a number. Horizontal lines take the form $y = $ a number.

Note that not all line equations are written in the form $y = mx + b$. In such cases, rewrite the equation so that it is expressed in the slope-intercept form. For example:

What is the slope-intercept form for a line with the equation $6x + 3y = 18$?

Rewrite the equation by solving for y as follows:

$$6x + 3y = 18$$
$$3y = 18 - 6x \qquad \text{(Subtract } 6x \text{ from both sides)}$$
$$y = 6 - 2x \qquad \text{(Divide both sides by 3)}$$
$$y = -2x + 6 \qquad \text{(Rewrite in } y = mx + b \text{ form)}$$

Horizontal and Vertical Lines

Horizontal and vertical lines are not expressed in the $y = mx + b$ form. Instead, they are expressed as simple, one-variable equations.

Horizontal lines are expressed in the form:
    $y = $ some number, such as $y = 3$ or $y = 5$.
Vertical lines are expressed in the form:
    $x = $ some number, such as $x = 4$ or $x = 7$.

All the points on a vertical line have the same x-coordinate, which is why its equation is defined only by x. Likewise, all the points on a horizontal line have the same y-coordinate, which is why its equation is defined only by y.

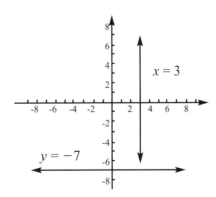

Step by Step: From 2 Points to a Line

If you are given any two points on a line, you should be able to write an equation for that line in the form $y = mx + b$. Here is the step-by-step method:

Find the equation of the line containing the points (3, 4) and (5, −2).

FIRST: Find the slope of the line by calculating the rise over the run.

The rise is determined by finding the difference between the y-coordinates, while the run is determined by finding the difference between the x-coordinates.

$$\frac{\text{rise}}{\text{run}} = \frac{y_1 - y_2}{x_1 - x_2} = \frac{-2 - 4}{5 - 3} = \frac{-6}{2} = -3$$ The slope of the line is negative three.

> To find the equation of a line, you should start by finding its slope.

SECOND: Plug the slope in for m in the slope-intercept equation.

$$y = -3x + b$$

THIRD: Solve for b, the y-intercept, by plugging one of the ordered pairs into the equation.

Plugging the point (3, 4) into the equation (3 for x and 4 for y) yields the following:

$$4 = -3(3) + b$$
$$4 = -9 + b$$ The y-intercept of the line is 13.
$$b = 13$$

FOURTH: Write the equation in the form $y = mx + b$.

$$y = -3x + 13$$ This is the equation of the line.

 Note that sometimes the GMAT will only give you one point on the line, along with the y-intercept. This is the same thing as giving you two points on the line, because the y-intercept is a point! A y-intercept of 4 is the same as the ordered pair (0, 4).

The Distance Between 2 Points

The distance between any two points in the coordinate plane can be calculated by using the Pythagorean Theorem. For example:

What is the distance between the points (1, 3) and (7, −5)?

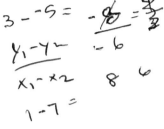

(1) Draw a right triangle connecting the points.

(2) Find the two legs of the triangle by calculating the rise and the run.

The *y*-coordinate changes from 3 to −5, a difference of 8 (the vertical leg).

The *x*-coordinate changes from 1 to 7, a difference of 6 (the horizontal leg).

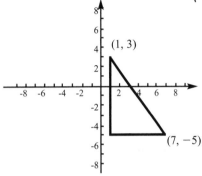

Draw a right triangle to find the distance between two points.

(3) Use the Pythagorean Theorem to calculate the length of the diagonal, which is the distance between the points.

$$6^2 + 8^2 = c^2$$
$$36 + 64 = c^2$$
$$100 = c^2$$
$$c = 10$$

The distance between the 2 points is 10 units.

Positive and Negative Quadrants

There are four quadrants in the coordinate plane, as shown in the diagram below.

Quadrant I contains only those points with a **positive** *x*-coordinate & a **positive** *y*-coordinate.

Quadrant II contains only those points with a **negative** *x*-coordinate & a **positive** *y*-coordinate.

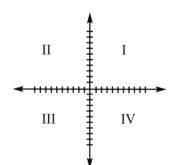

Quadrant III contains only those points with a **negative** *x*-coordinate & a **negative** *y*-coordinate.

Quadrant IV contains only those points with a **positive** *x*-coordinate & a **negative** *y*-coordinate.

You do not need to memorize the numbers of the quadrants. The numbers will always be provided for you.

The GMAT sometimes asks you to determine which quadrants a given line passes through. For example:

Which quadrants does the line $2x + y = 5$ pass through?

(1) First, rewrite the line in the form $y = mx + b$.

$$2x + y = 5$$
$$y = 5 - 2x$$
$$y = -2x + 5$$

(2) Then, find two points on your line by setting *x* and *y* equal to zero. These are the *x*- and *y*- intercepts.

$x = 0$	$y = 0$
$y = -2x + 5$	$0 = -2x + 5$
$y = -2(0) + 5$	$2x = 5$
$y = 5$	$x = 2.5$

The points $(0, 5)$ and $(2.5, 0)$ are both on the line.

(3) Finally, sketch the line, using the points you have identified.

If you plot $(0, 5)$ and $(2.5, 0)$ on the coordinate plane, you can connect them to see the position of the line.

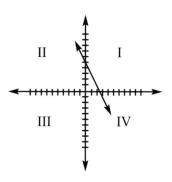

The line passes through quadrants I, II, and IV.

Perpendicular Bisectors

The perpendicular bisector of a line segment forms a 90° angle with the segment and divides the segment exactly in half. Questions about perpendicular bisectors are rare on the GMAT, but they do appear occasionally.

> **If the coordinates of _A_ are (2, 2) and the coordinates of _B_ are (0, −2), what is the equation of the perpendicular bisector of segment _AB_?**

The key to solving perpendicular bisector problems is remembering this property: the perpendicular bisector has the negative inverse slope of the line segment it bisects.

(1) Find the slope of segment _AB_.

$$\text{slope} = \frac{\text{rise}}{\text{run}} = \frac{y_1 - y_2}{x_1 - x_2} = \frac{2 - (-2)}{2 - 0} = \frac{4}{2} = 2$$

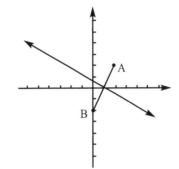

The slope of _AB_ is 2.

(2) Find the slope of the perpendicular bisector of _AB_.

Since perpendicular lines have negative inverse slopes, flip the fraction and change the sign.

The slope of the perpendicular bisector of _AB_ is $-\dfrac{1}{2}$.

Now we know that the equation of the perpendicular bisector has the following form:

$$y = -\frac{1}{2}x + b$$

However, we still need to find the value of _b_ (the _y_-intercept). To do this, we will need to find one point on the perpendicular bisector, and plug the coordinates of this point into the equation above.

<u>(3) Find the midpoint of *AB*.</u>

The perpendicular bisector passes through the midpoint of *AB*. Thus, if we find the midpoint of *AB*, we will have found a point on the perpendicular bisector. Organize a chart such as the one shown below to find the coordinates of the midpoint. Simply write the *x*- and *y*-coordinates of *A* and *B*. The coordinates of the midpoint will be the numbers right in between each pair of *x*- and *y*-coordinates.

	x	*y*
A	2	2
Midpoint	**1**	**0**
B	0	−2

To find the midpoint of a line segment, find the midpoints of the *x*- and *y*- coordinates separately.

<u>(4) Put the information together.</u>

To find the value of *b* (the *y*-intercept), substitute the coordinates of the midpoint for *x* and *y*.

$$0 = -\frac{1}{2}(1) + b$$

$$b = \frac{1}{2}$$

The perpendicular bisector of segment *AB* has the equation: $y = -\dfrac{1}{2}x + \dfrac{1}{2}$.

Problem Set

1. A line has the equation $y = 3x + 7$. At which point will this line intersect the y-axis?

2. A line has the equation $x = \dfrac{y}{80} - 20$. At which point will this line intersect the x-axis?

3   A line has the equation $x = -2y + z$. If $(3, 2)$ is a point on the line, what is z?

4. What are the equations for the four lines that form the boundaries of the shaded area in the figure shown?

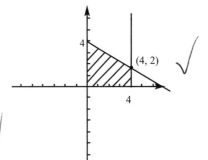

5. A line is represented by the equation $y = zx + 18$. If this line intersects the x-axis at $(-3, 0)$, what is z?

6. A line has a slope of 1/6 and intersects the x-axis at $(-24, 0)$. At which point does this line intersect the y-axis?

7. A line has a slope of 3/4 and intersects the point $(12, -39)$. At which point does this line intersect the x-axis?

8. The line represented by the equation $y = x$ is the perpendicular bisector of line segment AB. If A has the coordinates $(-3, 3)$, what are the coordinates of B?

9. The line represented by the equation $y = -2x + 6$ is the perpendicular bisector of the line segment AB. If A has the coordinates $(7, 2)$, what are the coordinates for B?

10. What are the coordinates for the point on Line AB (see figure) that is three times farther from A than B, and that is in between points A and B?

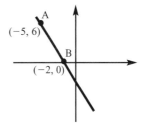

11. Which quadrants, if any, do not contain any points on the line represented by $x - y = 18$?

12. Which quadrants, if any, do not contain any points on the line represented by $\dfrac{x}{y} = 10$?

13. Which quadrants, if any, contain points on the line $y = \dfrac{x}{1000} + 1,000,000$?

14. Which quadrants, if any, contain points on the line represented by $\dfrac{x + 18}{y} = 2$?

15.   What is the equation of the line shown to the right?

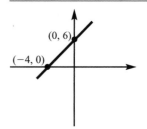

1. **(0, 7):** A line intersects the y-axis at the y-intercept. Since this equation is written in slope-intercept form, the y-intercept is easy to identify: 7. Thus, the line intersects the y-axis at the point (0, 7).

2. **(−20, 0) :** A line intersects the x-axis at the x-intercept, or when the y-coordinate is equal to zero. Substitute zero for y and solve for x:

$$x = 0 - 20$$
$$x = -20$$

3. **7:** Substitute the coordinates (3, 2) for x and y and solve for z.

$$3 = -2(2) + z$$
$$3 = -4 + z$$
$$z = 7$$

4. $x = 0$, $x = 4$, $y = 0$, **and** $y = -\dfrac{1}{2}x + 4$**:**

The shaded area is bounded by 2 vertical lines: $x = 0$ AND $x = 4$. Notice that all the points on each line share the same x-coordinate. The shaded area is bounded by 1 horizontal line, the x-axis. The equation for the x-axis is $y = 0$. Finally, the shaded area is bounded by a slanted line. To find the equation of this line, first calculate the slope, using two points on the line: (0, 4) and (4, 2).

$$\text{slope} = \frac{\text{rise}}{\text{run}} = \frac{4 - 2}{0 - 4} = \frac{2}{-4} = -\frac{1}{2}$$

We can read the y-intercept from the graph; it is the point at which the line crosses the y-axis, or 4.

Therefore, the equation of this line is $y = -\dfrac{1}{2}x + 4$.

5. **6:** Substitute the coordinates (3, 2) for x and y and solve for z.

$$0 = z(-3) + 18$$
$$3z = 18$$
$$z = 6$$

6. **(0, 4):** Use the information given to find the equation of the line:

$$y = \frac{1}{6}x + b$$

$$0 = \frac{1}{6}(-24) + b$$

$$0 = -4 + b$$
$$b = 4$$

The variable b represents the y-intercept. Therefore, the line intersects the y-axis at (0, 4).

7. **(40, 0):** Use the information given to find the equation of the line:

$$y = \frac{3}{4}x + b$$

$$-39 = \frac{3}{4}(-12) + b$$

$$-39 = -9 + b$$
$$b = -30$$

The line intersects the x-axis when $y = 0$. Set y equal to zero and solve for x:

$$0 = \frac{3}{4}x - 30$$

$$\frac{3}{4}x = 30$$

$$x = 40$$

The line intersects the x-axis at $(0, 40)$.

8. **(3, −3):** Perpendicular lines have negative inverse slopes. Therefore, if $y = x$ is perpendicular to segment AB, we know that the slope of the perpendicular bisector is 1, and therefore the slope of segment AB is -1. The line containing segment AB takes the form of $y = -x + b$. To find the value of b, substitute the coordinates of A, $(-3, 3)$, into the equation:

$$3 = -(-3) + b$$
$$b = 0$$

The line containing segment AB is $y = -x$.

Find the point at which the perpendicular bisector intersects AB by setting the two equations, $y = x$ and $y = -x$, equal to each other:

$$x = -x$$
$$x = 0; \; y = 0$$

The two lines intersect at $(0, 0)$, which is the midpoint of AB.

Use a chart to find the coordinates of B.

	x	y
A	−3	3
Midpoint	0	0
B	**3**	**−3**

9. **(−1, −2):** If $y = -2x + 6$ is the perpendicular bisector of segment AB, then the line containing segment AB must have a slope of .5 (the negative inverse of -2). We can represent this line with the equation $y = .5x + b$. Substitute the coordinates (7, 2) into the equation to find the value of b.

     $2 = .5(7) + b$.
     $b = -1.5$

The line containing AB is $y = .5x − 1.5$.

Find the point at which the perpendicular bisector intersects AB by setting the two equations, $y = -2x + 6$ and $y = .5x − 1.5$, equal to each other.

     $-2x + 6 = .5x − 1.5$
        $2.5x = 7.5$
          $x = 3; y = 0$

The two lines intersect at (3, 0), which is the midpoint of AB.

	x	y
A	7	2
Midpoint	3	0
B	−1	−2

Use a chart to find the coordinates of B.

10. **(−2.75, 1.5):** The point in question is 3 times farther from A than it is from B. We can represent this fact by labeling the point $3x$ units from A and x units from B, as shown, giving us a total distance of $4x$ between the two points. If we drop vertical lines from the point and from A to the x-axis, we get 2 similar triangles, the smaller of which is a quarter of the larger. (We can get this relationship from the fact that the larger triangle's hypotenuse is 4 times larger than the hypotenuse of the smaller triangle.)

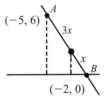

The horizontal distance between points A and B is 3 units (from -2 to -5). Therefore, $4x = 3$, and $x = .75$. The horizontal distance from B to the point is x, or .75 units. The x-coordinate of the point is .75 away from -2, or -2.75.

The vertical distance between points A and B is 6 units (from 0 to 6). Therefore, $4x = 6$, and $x = 1.5$. The vertical distance from B to the point is x, or 1.5 units. The y-coordinate of the point is 1.5 away from 0, or 1.5.

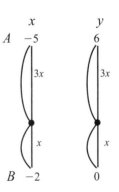

11. **II:** First, rewrite the line in slope-intercept form:
     $y = x − 18$
Find the intercepts by setting x to zero and y to zero:
     $y = 0 − 18$ $0 = x − 18$
     $y = -18$ $x = 18$
Plot the points: (0, −18), and (18, 0). From the sketch, we can see that the line does not pass through quadrant II.

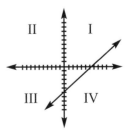

12. **II and IV:** First, rewrite the line in slope-intercept form:

$$y = \frac{x}{10}$$

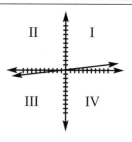

Notice from the equation that the *y*-intercept of the line is (0,0). This means that the line crosses the *y*-intercept at the origin, so the *x*- and *y*-intercepts are the same. To find another point on the line, substitute any convenient number for *x*; in this case, 10 would be a convenient, or "smart," number.

$$y = \frac{10}{10} = 1 \qquad \text{The point (10, 1) is on the line.}$$

Plot the points: (0, 0) and (10, 1). From the sketch, we can see that the line does not pass through quadrants II and IV.

13. **I, II, and III:** First, rewrite the line in slope-intercept form:

$$y = \frac{x}{1000} + 1{,}000{,}000$$

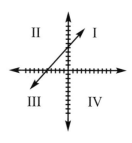

Find the intercepts by setting *x* to zero and *y* to zero:

$$0 = \frac{x}{1000} + 1{,}000{,}000 \qquad y = \frac{0}{1000} + 1{,}000{,}000$$

$$x = -1{,}000{,}000{,}000 \qquad y = 1{,}000{,}000$$

Plot the points: (−1,000,000,000, 0) and (0, 1,000,000). From the sketch, we can see that the line passes through quadrants I, II, and III.

14. **I, II, and III:** First, rewrite the line in slope-intercept form:

$$y = \frac{x}{2} + 9$$

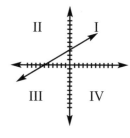

Find the intercepts by setting *x* to zero and *y* to zero:

$$0 = \frac{x}{2} + 9 \qquad\qquad y = \frac{0}{2} + 9$$

$$x = -18 \qquad\qquad y = 9$$

Plot the points: (−18, 0) and (0, 9). From the sketch, we can see that the line passes through quadrants I, II, and III.

15. $y = \dfrac{3}{2}x + 6$: First, calculate the slope of the line:

$$\text{slope} = \frac{\text{rise}}{\text{run}} = \frac{6 - 0}{0 - (-4)} = \frac{6}{4} = \frac{3}{2}$$

We can see from the graph that the line crosses the y-axis at $(0,6)$. The equation of the line is:

$$y = \frac{3}{2}x + 6$$

Chapter 6
of
GEOMETRY

STRATEGIES FOR DATA SUFFICIENCY

In This Chapter . . .

- Rephrasing: Access Useful Formulas and Rules
- Sample Rephrasings for Challenging Problems

Rephrasing: Access Useful Formulas and Rules

Geometry data sufficiency problems require you to identify the rules and formulas of geometry. For example, if you are given a problem about a circle, you should immediately access the rules and formulas you know that involve circles:

> Area of a circle = πr^2
> Circumference of a circle = $2\pi r$
> A central angle describes an arc that is proportional to a fractional part of 360°.
> An inscribed angle describes an arc that is proportional to a fractional part of 180°.

If *B* is the center of the circle to the right, what is the length of line segment *AC*?

(1) The area of sector *ABCD* is 4π
(2) The circumference of the circle is 8π

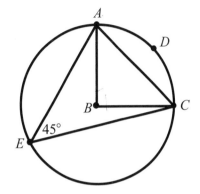

A   Statement (1) ALONE is sufficient, but statement (2) alone is not sufficient.
B   Statement (2) ALONE is sufficient, but statement (1) alone is not sufficient.
C   BOTH statements TOGETHER are sufficient, but NEITHER statement ALONE is sufficient.
D   EACH statement ALONE is sufficient.
E   Statements (1) and (2) together are NOT sufficient.

Always start by focusing on the question itself. Do not jump to the statements before first attempting to rephrase the question into something easier.

The diagram shows that ∠*AEC* (an inscribed angle that intercepts arc *ADC*) is 45°.

Therefore, using the relationship between an inscribed angle and a central angle, we know that ∠*ABC* (a central angle that also intercepts arc *ADC*) must be 90°.

Thus, triangle *ABC* is a right triangle.

The question asks us to find the length of line segment *AC*, which is the hypotenuse of the right triangle. In order to find the length of hypotenuse *AC*, we must determine the length of the legs of the triangle. Notice that each leg of the triangle (*BA* and *BC*) is a radius of the circle.

Thus, this question can be rephrased: **What is the radius of the circle?**

To solve Data Sufficiency problems in Geometry, apply the formulas and rules you have memorized.

The 2 circle formulas you should know that include the radius are the formula for area and the formula for circumference.

Statement (1) tells us the area of a sector of the circle. Since the sector described is one quarter of the circle, we will be able to determine the area of the entire circle using a proportion. Given the area of the circle, we can find the radius.

Thus, statement (1) alone is sufficient to answer our rephrased question.

Statement (2) tells us the circumference of the circle. Using the formula for circumference, we can determine the radius of the circle.

Thus, statement (2) alone is sufficient to answer our rephrased question.

The answer to this data sufficiency problem is (D): EACH statement ALONE is sufficient.

Try to determine whether each statement provides enough information to answer your *rephrased* question.

the new standard

Rephrasing: Challenge Short Set

At the very end of this book, you will find lists of GEOMETRY problems that have appeared on past official GMAT exams. These lists reference problems from *The Official Guide for GMAT Review, 11th Edition* and *The Official Guide for GMAT Quantitative Review* (the questions contained therein are the property of The Graduate Management Admission Council, which is not affiliated in any way with Manhattan GMAT).

As you work through the Data Sufficiency problems listed at the end of this book, be sure to focus on *rephrasing*. If possible, try to *rephrase* each question into its simplest form *before* looking at the two statements. In order to rephrase, focus on figuring out the specific information that is absolutely necessary to answer the question. After rephrasing the question, you should also try to *rephrase* each of the two statements, if possible. Rephrase each statement by simplifying the given information into its most basic form.

In order to help you practice rephrasing, we have taken the most difficult Data Sufficiency problems on *The Official Guide* problem list (these are the problem numbers listed in the "Challenge Short Set" on page 97) and have provided you with our own sample rephrasings for each question and statement. In order to evaluate how effectively you are using the rephrasing strategy, you can compare your rephrased questions and statements to our own rephrasings that appear below. Questions and statements that are significantly rephrased appear in **bold**.

Rephrasings from *The Official Guide For GMAT Review, 11th Edition*

The questions and statements that appear below are only our *rephrasings*. The original questions and statements can be found by referencing the problem numbers below in the Data Sufficiency section of *The Official Guide for GMAT Review, 11th edition* (pages 278-290).

<u>Note</u>: Problem numbers preceded by "D" refer to questions in the Diagnostic Test chapter of *The Official Guide for GMAT Review, 11th edition* (pages 24-25).

D39. x-intercept is the point on line where $y = 0$.

   At point $(x, 0)$ on line k, is x positive?

   (1) Slope = distance between any 2 points on line: $-5 = \dfrac{rise}{run} = \dfrac{y_2 - y_1}{x_2 - x_1}$

   Plug in two points on line k: $(x, 0)$ and $(-5, r)$

   $$-5 = \frac{r - 0}{-5 - x} = \frac{r}{-5 - x}$$

   $$25 + 5x = r$$

   $$x = \frac{r - 25}{5}$$

   x is positive if r is greater than 25

   (2) $r > 0$

D48.

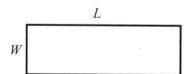

   What is $2L + 2W$?   OR   **What is $L + W$?**

   (1)

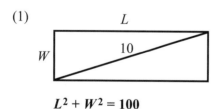

   $L^2 + W^2 = 100$

   (2) $LW = 48$

15. Recall the signs of coordinates in each quadrant:

QUADRANT	a	b
I	positive	positive
II	negative	positive
III	negative	negative
IV	positive	negative

What are the signs of a and b?

(1) a is negative; b is positive

(2) a is negative; b is positive

38. **Is the total thickness of the first 10 volumes less than or equal to x?**

(1) $x = 50$ centimeters

(2) 12 volumes are a total of 60 centimeters thick.

41. **What is the diameter of each can?**

(1) $r = 4$
   $d = 8$

(2) $6d = 48$
   $d = 8$

51. There are $180°$ in a triangle: $x + y + z = 180$
   $z = 180 - (x + y)$
What is the value of $x + y$?

(1) $x + y = 139$

(2) $y + z = 108$

113. **What is the length of one side of triangle D?**

(1) **The length of the height of triangle D is 3.**

(2) **The length of the base of triangle D is $\frac{8}{3}$.**

117. **What is the ratio of $\dfrac{KN}{MN}$?**

(1) $KM + MN = 15$

(2) $MN = 1.5(KN)$

$$\frac{KN}{MN} = \frac{1}{1.5}$$

136. $C = 2\pi r$

What is the radius?   OR

Arc lengths are determined by central angles.

Thus, the length of arc $XYZ = \dfrac{90}{360} = \dfrac{1}{4}$ of the circumference.

What is the length of arc XYZ?

(1) Triangle OXZ is a 45 - 45 - 90 triangle with sides in the ratio of $1: 1: \sqrt{2}$, and each of the shorter legs is a radius of the circle. Thus, the perimeter is $r + r + \sqrt{2}r$. Using the value for the perimeter given in statement (1), solve for the radius:

$r = 10$

(2) arc $XYZ = 5\pi$

140. The distance of a point to the origin can be determined with the Pythagorean Theorem.

Does $r^2 + s^2 = u^2 + v^2$?

(1) $s = -r + 1$

(2) $v = 1 - s$ AND $u = 1 - r$

(COMBINED)
$v = 1 - (-r + 1)$ AND $u = 1 - r$
$v = r + 2$

Using substitution, we can answer the rephrased question.

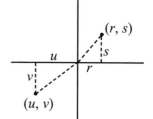

152. The large triangle (*PQR*) is inscribed in a semi-circle, and its hypotenuse (*PR*) is the diameter of the semi-circle. Therefore, triangle *PQR* is a right triangle; its right angle is at point *Q*.

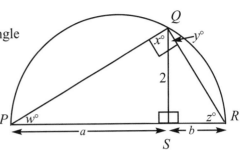

Now we have one large right triangle (*PQR*) and two small right triangles (*PSQ* and *RSQ*). Notice that triangle *PQR* and triangle *PSQ* share two angles in common (angle *w* and a right angle). Since the sum of the angles in any triangle is 180 degrees, the third angle in each of these triangles must also be congruent. Therefore, these triangles are similar.

The same logic applies for triangle *PQR* and triangle *RSQ*. These two triangles are similar as well.

Since the large triangle *PQR* is similar to both of the smaller triangles, *PSQ* and *RSQ*, then these two smaller triangles must also be similar to each other. Therefore, knowing any pair of corresponding sides will give us the proportions of the other pairs of corresponding sides.

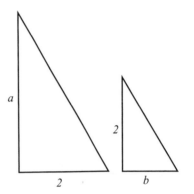

What is *a*?   OR   What is *b*?

(1) $a = 4$

(2) $b = 1$

Rephrasings from *The Official Guide for GMAT Quantitative Review*

The questions and statements that appear below are only our *rephrasings*. The original questions and statements can be found by referencing the problem numbers below in the Data Sufficiency section of *The Official Guide for GMAT Quantitative Review* (pages 149-157).

58.   Circumference of a circle = $2\pi r$

Number of rotations = $\dfrac{100}{2\pi r}$

What is the value of r?

(1) diameter = 0.5 meter

(2) speed = 20 rotations per minute

70.   **What is the measure of angle ABC?   OR**
       What are the measures of ABX, XBY, and YBC?

(1) $ABX = XBY$ **AND** $XBY = YBC$
       $ABX = XBY = YBC$

(2) $ABX = 40°$

87.   TUV is a 45 - 45 - 90 right triangle. RUV is a 30 - 60 - 90 right triangle.
       TU = RS

What is the length of the base of each of these triangles?   OR
What is the length of the hypotenuse these triangles share?   OR
(BEST): What is the length of any side in either triangle?
**Note that knowing 1 side allows us to solve for all other sides.

(1) TU = 10 m

(2) RV = 5 m

91.   Let r = the radius of the smaller region.
       Let R = the radius of the larger region.
       What is R?

(1) $\pi r^2 + \pi R^2 = 90\pi$
       $r^2 + R^2 = 90$

(2) $R = 3r$

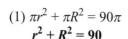

109. **What is lw?**

(1) $l + w = 6$
$(l + w)^2 = 36$
$\mathbf{l^2 + 2lw + w^2 = 36}$

(2) $\mathbf{l^2 + w^2 = 20}$

(COMBINED)
$$l^2 + 2lw + w^2 = 36$$
$$- \quad l^2 \qquad + w^2 = 20$$

$$2lw \quad = 16$$
$$\mathbf{lw = 8}$$

117. Name angles y and z as shown in the figure to the right.

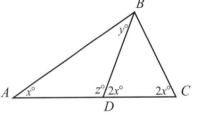

$2x + z = 180$ OR $z = 180 - 2x$
$x + y + z = 180$ OR $z = 180 - (x + y)$
Therefore, $2x = x + y$ OR $x = y$. Thus, $AD = BD$.

We also know that $BD = BC$.
Therefore, $AD = BD = BC$.

What is the length of BC, BD, or AD?

(1) $AD = 6$

(2) $x = 36$

Chapter 7
of
GEOMETRY

OFFICIAL GUIDE
PROBLEM SETS

In This Chapter . . .

- Geometry Problem Solving List from *The Official Guides*
- Geometry Data Sufficiency List from *The Official Guides*

Practicing with REAL GMAT Problems

Now that you have completed your study of GEOMETRY, it is time to test your skills on problems that have actually appeared on real GMAT exams over the past several years.

The problem sets that follow are composed of questions from two books published by the Graduate Management Admission Council® (the organization that develops the official GMAT exam):

The Official Guide for GMAT Review, 11th Edition &
The Official Guide for GMAT Quantitative Review

These two books contain quantitative questions that have appeared on past official GMAT exams. (The questions contained therein are the property of The Graduate Management Admission Council, which is not affiliated in any way with Manhattan GMAT.)

Although the questions in the Official Guides have been "retired" (they will not appear on future official GMAT exams), they are great practice questions.

In order to help you practice effectively, we have categorized every problem in The Official Guides by topic and subtopic. On the following pages, you will find two categorized lists:

(1) **Problem Solving:** Lists all Problem Solving GEOMETRY questions contained in *The Official Guides* and categorizes them by subtopic.

(2) **Data Sufficiency:** Lists all Data Sufficiency GEOMETRY questions contained in *The Official Guides* and categorizes them by subtopic.

Note: Each book in Manhattan GMAT's 7-book preparation series contains its own *Official Guide* lists that pertain to the specific topic of that particular book. If you complete all the practice problems contained on the *Official Guide* lists in the back of each of the 7 Manhattan GMAT preparation books, you will have completed every single question published in *The Official Guides*. At that point, you should be ready to take your Official GMAT exam!

Problem Solving

from *The Official Guide for GMAT Review, 11th edition* (pages 20-23 & 152-186) and *The Official Guide for GMAT Quantitative Review* (pages 62-85)

Note: Problem numbers preceded by "D" refer to questions in the Diagnostic Test chapter of *The Official Guide for GMAT Review, 11th edition* (pages 20-23).

Solve each of the following problems in a notebook, making sure to demonstrate how you arrived at each answer by showing all of your work and computations. If you get stuck on a problem, look back at the GEOMETRY strategies and content contained in this guide to assist you.

CHALLENGE SHORT SET

This set contains the more difficult geometry problems from each of the content areas.
> *11th edition*: D10, D20, D22, 30, 36, 45, 60, 89, 152, 176, 191, 206, 226, 227, 238, 248
> *Quantitative Review*: 123, 139, 175

FULL PROBLEM SET

Polygons
> *11th edition*: 3, 13, 16, 105, 112, 134, 238
> *Quantitative Review*: 12, 22, 139, 175

Triangles and Diagonals
> *11th edition*: D19, 45, 145, 147, 152, 176, 222

Circles and Cylinders
> *11th edition*: D5, D20, D22, 30, 160, 191, 206
> *Quantitative Review*: 31, 141

Lines and Angles
> *11th edition*: D10, 51, 60, 226
> *Quantitative Review*: 28

Coordinate Plane
> *11th edition*: 7, 23, 36, 89, 199, 227, 248
> *Quantitative Review*: 19, 123

Data Sufficiency

from *The Official Guide for GMAT Review, 11th edition* (pages 24-25 & 278-290) and *The Official Guide for GMAT Quantitative Review* (pages 149-157)

<u>Note</u>: Problem numbers preceded by "D" refer to questions in the Diagnostic Test chapter of *The Official Guide for GMAT Review, 11th edition* (pages 24-25).

Solve each of the following problems in a notebook, making sure to demonstrate how you arrived at each answer by showing all of your work and computations. If you get stuck on a problem, look back at the GEOMETRY strategies and content contained in this guide to assist you.

Practice REPHRASING both the questions and the statements by using your knowledge of geometric formulas and concepts. The majority of data sufficiency problems can be rephrased; however, if you have difficulty rephrasing a problem, try testing numbers to solve it.

It is especially important that you familiarize yourself with the directions for data sufficiency problems, and that you memorize the 5 fixed answer choices that accompany all data sufficiency problems.

CHALLENGE SHORT SET
This set contains the more difficult geometry problems from each of the content areas.
> *11th edition*: D39, D48, 15, 38, 41, 51, 113, 117, 136, 140, 152
> *Quantitative Review*: 58, 70, 87, 91, 109, 117

FULL PROBLEM SET
Polygons
> *11th edition*: D48, 38, 47, 102, 117
> *Quantitative Review*: 4, 59, 84

Triangles and Diagonals
> *11th edition*: D28, 27, 32, 51, 108, 113, 152
> *Quantitative Review*: 19, 64, 87, 109, 117

Circles and Cylinders
> *11th edition*: D36, 39, 41, 76, 86, 136
> *Quantitative Review*: 57, 58, 91, 95

Lines and Angles
> *11th edition*: 6, 23, 72
> *Quantitative Review*: 70

Coordinate Plane
> *11th edition*: D39, 15, 78, 85, 124, 140
> *Quantitative Review*: 14